STEVE JOBS MONOGRAPH

edited by B.C. Wallin

The MONOGRAPH

STEVE JOBS MONOGRAPH is dedicated to the premise that to understand a work as greater than the sum of its parts, one must understand and appreciate each of the parts.

This volume is focused on the 2015 film *Steve Jobs*.

Plot Summary

Backstage before three product launches in 1984, 1988, and 1998, **Steve Jobs** tinkers with preparations and verbally spars with important people in his life. Apple Computers co-founder **Steve Wozniak** wants Jobs to acknowledge the people whose work is the foundation of his genius public persona. Ex-flame **Chrisann Brennan** wants Job to acknowledge and financially support his daughter. **Lisa Brennan-Jobs** wants her father to see her. Apple CEO **John Sculley** wants to be Jobs' partner, though he finds himself increasingly at odds with the visionary's non-traditional ideas and mercurial personality. Engineer **Andy Hertzfeld** is the subject of Jobs' ire when he struggles to solve a bug before the launch of the Macintosh and later when he overrides Jobs' cruel parenting decisions. And Apple head of marketing **Joanna Hoffman** observes it all, standing by Jobs while trying to help him see reality.

Selected Credits

Cast

Steve Jobs	Michael Fassbender
Joanna Hoffman	Kate Winslet
Steve Wozniak	Seth Rogen
John Sculley	Jeff Daniels
Andy Hertzfeld	Michael Stuhlbarg
Chrisann Brennan	Katherine Waterston
Lisa Brennan (19)	Perla Haney-Jardine
Lisa Brennan (9)	Ripley Sobo
Lisa Brennan (5)	Makenzie Moss
Andrea Cunningham	Sarah Snook
Joel Pforzheimer	John Ortiz
Avie Tevanian	Adam Shapiro

Crew

Directed by	Danny Boyle
Screenplay by	Aaron Sorkin
Based on the Book by	Walter Isaacson
Produced by	Mark Gordon, p.g.a.
	Guymon Casady, p.g.a.
	Scott Rudin, p.g.a.
	Danny Boyle, p.g.a.
	Christian Colson, p.g.a.
Executive Producers	Bernard Bellew
	Bryan Zuriff
	Eli Bush
Director of Photography	Alwin Küchler, BSC
Production Designer	Guy Hendrix Dyas
Editor	Elliot Graham, ACE
Costume Designer	Suttirat Larlarb
Music By	Daniel Pemberton
Casting By	Francine Maisler, CSA

Contents

Production

by B.C. Wallin

On October 5, 2011, death, as it must to all men, came to Steven Paul Jobs. He was behind the devices that played our music, created our work, stored our memories, and connected us to others, and at the age of 56, he died from complications of pancreatic cancer. Only two days later, *Deadline* reported that a biopic, as it must for all icons, was coming for Steve Jobs.

Jobs' biography hadn't even hit shelves when Sony Pictures agreed to pay $1-3 million to adapt it into a film. Walter Isaacson, past managing editor of *TIME* magazine and biographer of Albert Einstein, Benjamin Franklin, and now Jobs, had met with the Apple co-founder over 40 times and conducted over 100 interviews with the significant figures in his life. While Jobs lay on his deathbed, Sony CEO Michael Lynton and producer Mark Gordon got the chance to read his book early, according to *The Hollywood Reporter*. At the time, the only Steve Jobs biopic was the 1999 made-for-

TV movie *Pirates of Silicon Valley*, which had aired on TNT.[1]

In black turtleneck and rimless glasses, Jobs was the iconic face behind the iPod, iPhone, and Macintosh — he had made his identity synonymous with Apple's, as he led product launch keynotes with the kind of pomp and spectacle that would be imitated by tech competitors and entertainment studios alike. His dramatic rise and fall and rise again had played out on a global stage. Isaacson's biography, published on October 24, 2011, and simply titled *Steve Jobs*, sold 379,000 copies in its first week on shelves and would go on to sell over three million copies in the U.S. alone — the film project, it would seem, was a no-brainer.

The day after the biography went on sale, the *Los Angeles Times* reported that Sony wanted Aaron Sorkin to be the one to adapt it — he was, after all, the Oscar-winning screenwriter behind Sony's last great tech biopic, *The Social Network*, about Mark Zuckerberg, CEO and co-founder of the company then known as Facebook. Under David Fincher's helming, Sorkin had done the seemingly impossible, turning legal depositions about stock dilution and IP infringement into a cool movie. Again, a no-brainer.

---

[1] Per star Noah Wyle in *Fortune*, Jobs called Wyle to tell him, "I hated the movie, I hated the script, I think if you had spent a little more time and a little more money and maybe a little more attention to detail, you could have had something there. But you were good." Jobs then invited Wyle to Apple's 1999 Macworld convention where the *ER* actor would come onstage in turtleneck, jeans, and glasses, reprising the role of the then-interim CEO, before Jobs, dressed identically, came out to show he was in on the joke.

Sorkin would be the first to tell you he was not a Steve Jobs fanatic, nor did he fully understand the phenomenon. Writing for *Newsweek*, Sorkin described his main interactions with Jobs in three phone calls: the first, to thank the writer for kind words he'd said about Jobs' products,[2] the second, to tell him not to be discouraged about a show of his getting cancelled — Sorkin was shocked someone as busy as Steve Jobs would take the time to console a writer he barely knew — and the third, to see if Sorkin would consider writing a PIXAR movie. On the final call, Sorkin said he wouldn't know how to do the job: "I don't think I can make inanimate objects talk." As Sorkin recalls, Jobs responded, "Once you make them talk, they won't be inanimate."

The screenwriter would spend months researching and conceptualizing the biopic before he found the two things nobody else had. Unlike Isaacson, Sorkin was able to get access to Steve's daughter, Lisa Brennan-Jobs, who hadn't wanted to speak about her father while he was alive. "She was able to tell stories about her father that weren't necessarily flattering stories, but she would tell the story and then show me how you could see he really did love her," Sorkin told *Business Insider*. And unlike a competing Jobs biopic announced within six months of Sony's by a first-time producer from a real estate background, Sorkin had come up with a non-traditional biopic structure: the film, instead of being a "cradle-to-

---

[2] In response to the question "Mac or PC?" Sorkin had answered, "Everything I've ever written, I've written on a Mac."

grave," Wikipedia entry of a movie, would take place in relatively real time in the 40-or-so minutes leading up to three significant product launches in Jobs' life.

Over the next two and a half years, the project would be plagued by leaks, hacks, stories, and scandals. Fincher was courted to re-partner with Sorkin and direct, but left over budget concerns, among other issues. Leonardo DiCaprio and Christian Bale both came very close to starring as the Apple visionary, but dropped out — DiCaprio was focused on *The Revenant* and Bale said he couldn't get a handle on the materials, but per an unnamed "key player" in the film quoted by *The Hollywood Reporter*, Jobs' widow, Laurene Powell Jobs tried to dissuade them, calling them both and saying "Don't do it." Sony's actor wishlist included Matt Damon, Ben Affleck, and Bradley Cooper. Sorkin suggested Tom Cruise (a fun exercise to imagine, though nothing much came of the idea). Danny Boyle came onboard as Fincher's replacement and chose Michael Fassbender for the title role — Boyle saw something "Jobsian" in him, describing it in production notes as "this incredible intensity about the application of what he's doing." But without Fincher onboard or a household name as the lead, Sony got cold feet and put the film in turnaround, for another studio to buy it.

There's another version of this story. One with North Korean hackers, private emails, and a press hungry for every bit of behind-the-scenes gossip and unvarnished truth. There's a version that hangs the dirty laundry of anyone unfortunate enough to have an email in Sony

Picture Entertainment's servers out to dry. Hackers purportedly retaliated in advance of a satirical representation of Kim Jong Un in Seth Rogen and Evan Goldberg's *The Interview*, dumping troves of stolen emails, documents, home addresses, and other sensitive information online (still, at time of publication, available to anyone who chooses to go looking). *Steve Jobs* got caught in the crossfire, and so did executives, cast, and crew at all levels of production. In 2014 and the years since, apologies were made, relationships were broken, and we consumed. Sorkin wondered in an op-ed what a world would look like that had invoked NATO's principle of collective defense, Article 5 — if it had been agreed that an attack on one is an attack on all, and if we had chosen instead to leave those stolen messages unread. We can choose how to tell this story.

It wasn't long after being dropped by Sony — just 5 days in *The Hollywood Reporter*'s narrative — that the project was picked up by Universal Pictures with Boyle to direct and Fassbender to star. By the end of November 2014, the film had a home, and by late January 2015, *Deadline* reported, the cast was finalized and shooting was underway. If the pre-production narrative was one of in-fighting, indecision, and everything that could fall apart doing so, production was a story of collaboration, fluidity, and endless challenge.

The work at hand was to create a triptych of mostly continuous backstage dramas driven almost entirely by dialogue, and to make it interesting. Boyle described the talkativeness of Sorkin's screenplay as a provocation:

"It's a grand act," he told *Interview Magazine,*

> "what do you do with that? I loved it. It's like nothing I'd ever done before and it's an extraordinary opportunity for actors. You've got to get great actors who have the right attitude and can sense his rhythm. Once you get his rhythm — and I hesitate to say this — it does itself."

All of the performers would have an overwhelming amount of dialogue to learn, but none more than Fassbender, who would tell *TIME* magazine that memorizing Sorkin's script was harder than memorizing Shakespeare (he starred in *Macbeth*, directed by Justin Kurzel, the same year and would be at its Cannes premiere the month after *Steve Jobs* shooting wrapped). Filming between January and April of 2015, Fassbender had around 200 pages of twisty, verbose dialogue to memorize — to give him a fighting chance, and in keeping with Boyle's background in theatre, the production would be broken up and supported by rehearsals.

"Thankfully, Danny had the foresight to build in a rehearsal period between the filming of each act," Fassbender says in the film's production notes, "which is very rare; that never happens." Unlike most movies, *Steve Jobs* would be shot mainly in sequence (in the order the scenes follow in the movie). Unlike most movies, *Steve Jobs* would have three weeks of rehearsal before shooting commenced, with filming pausing for another two weeks of rehearsal between Acts I and II and again between Acts II and III, as if the cast and crew were making three 40-minute movies in consecutive production. "I will be eternally grateful," says Fassbender, "because I would never have been able to film at this pace without that." Boyle described Fassbender's process to *Interview Magazine*:

> "The way he did it was he learned the whole thing and then polished Act I just before we started. Then, when we were doing Part One, he was polishing Act II at home in the evenings, so he was under tremendous pressure. When we were doing Act II, he was polishing Act III at home and at weekends. When we got to Part Three, he had nothing to polish in the evenings and I think you can see it in his performance. He's so relaxed in that third part, whereas in the early parts, he's kind of battling. It suits the character as well, because he's battling everyone who stands in his way. There's an aggression, a punkishness about him, which is horrible and also dynamic."

During the rehearsal period, the real-life personalities behind the film came in to meet with the actors and share their perspectives. Former Apple CEO John Sculley came to rehearsals and helped Jeff Daniels understand the person he would be playing. Former Apple marketing executive Joanna Hoffman spoke to the *Steve Jobs* team, including actress Kate Winslet, who was able to spend significant time with her, hearing how she spoke, seeing how she dressed, and understanding the push-and-pull of Jobs' closest work relationships. Apple co-founder Steve Wozniak, who had initially been hired by Sony as a consultant on the project, came to the rehearsals — Seth Rogen met the man he would be portraying then. Michael Stuhlbarg also got to meet Jobs' friend and key Apple engineer Andy Hertzfeld before playing him. During his research process, Sorkin had spoken with all of the real-life figures, along with

Lisa (played by Makenzie Moss, Ripley Sobo, and Perla Haney-Jardine across the three acts) and her mother Chrisann Brennan (played by Katherine Waterston). Haney-Jardine noted that during rehearsals, she was able to learn from her younger counterparts, picking up quirks and mannerisms, to create a throughline in their relay race performance as Jobs' daughter.

Rehearsal was a time to learn, familiarize, and experiment. Sharing the most scenes of the movie with Fassbender, Winslet would become an important collaborator for him in the process.[3] In *Inside Jobs*, a featurette of behind-the-scenes material, she tells a story of Fassbender coming into a day of rehearsals and saying he would try a bunch of weird things. Out of this experimentation came a moment of physical performance in Act III, where Jobs does yoga as Hoffman shares maybe the first good news of the film with him: he's finally made a successful product. The movements weren't part of Boyle's plans, but they developed organically out of the process of trial and error. "I think what Danny values least is conformity," says editor Elliot Graham, "he does not want you to follow his lead, he wants you to bring something to the table."

The process helped in finding performance, but it was also integral in developing blocking and movement. "We approached rehearsal and filming in a way that I hoped

---

[3] Winslet told *Vulture* she'd learned of the role from her hair-and-makeup artist on another project and pursued it by emailing a picture of herself in a Hoffman-esque wig to producer Scott Rudin, no subject line. Three and a half weeks later, she was in rehearsals in San Francisco.

would liberate the actors physically," Boyle says in production notes, "I didn't want to create spaces on set that were confined, but rather provide a sense of freedom and openness." Beyond a natural relationship with the language, rehearsal was a period of preparation for a shoot that would be almost entirely on-location. In *Inside Jobs*, Sorkin says, "We would do something I've never seen in rehearsal of a movie. We would do entire run-throughs with the set taped off on the floor: we would do an entire first act run-through, an entire second act run-through, an entire third act..." The actors were free to explore while preparing for the real shooting spaces. "We kind of just walked through the scenes," says Rogen, describing the process. "It's a big room with chairs and tables so you can kind of set up a little mock-up of wherever the scenes are taking place — if it's a walk-and-talk, we'll literally just walk in a circle."

Shooting in and around San Francisco, "the Bethlehem of the modern world, of the digital age," per Boyle, the film was mainly confined to the three venues of the plot's three product launches. Act I shot in Cupertino, in the Flint Center for the Performing Arts, where the Macintosh was actually introduced in 1984, with additional photography in the real-life garage where Jobs sat and (in the words of the script) "invented the future" with Wozniak. Production would pull from real, physical touchstones as much as possible, while also taking necessary steps to recreate a decades-old world, both in actuality and aesthetic.

Starting in Flint with a blank canvas of bland, white

walls backstage, the production transformed the venue's hallways and rooms with a new color palette of "institutional green and gold," per assistant art director Susie Alegria in the Art Directors Guild publication *Perspective*. Red exit signs backstage were not turned off, but they were swapped out for green, saving red as the primary color for Act II. "We used late 1970s colors like mustard and green to dress and paint Flint Hall, which worked well to show that in contrast the Macintosh was a thing of the future," said production designer Guy Hendrix Dyas in a *Below the Line* profile.

"Everything about the 1984 launch represents looking to the future," says costume designer Suttirat Larlarb in the production notes. "So the clothes of the people presenting the Macintosh, as well as the clothes of the people who are reacting to the presentation, have to be on this continuum where that machine is the most futuristic thing in the room." The auditorium on the De Anza College campus was packed with extras dressed and styled to match the period. A *CNET* writer who was unable to join the crowd inside the auditorium described a horde of hopeful extras that had waited in line since around 5 a.m., including "people clad in acid-washed denim jackets and mom jeans" and "more oversized blazers with shoulder pads than I've seen in one place in my life." A writer for *MacWorld* did report making it into the venue as an extra, writing that "For most of the shoot, a beige bag was perched on a pedestal in the center of the stage." And while officially released B-roll footage does show Fassbender running through the presentation onstage, he would never present the Macintosh to a crowd in the finished film.[4]

Steve Jobs is a movie of build-up (notice how long it takes for Jobs to be introduced by name onstage), spending most of its time in the rarely seen backstage spaces and almost none in the polished keynotes synonymous with Apple and Jobs. "I'm more naturally a playwright," says Sorkin in production notes, "I'm most comfortable in claustrophobic places, with a ticking clock in a clearly defined space." Production occupied Flint for 22 days, with 11 of those days spent filming and the rest of the time used for set-up and rehearsals, according to the center's event coordinator Rhonda Doyle, quoted in the *Los Angeles Times*.

After their first break for rehearsals, the team moved on to shooting Act II, centered around Jobs' first major product launch after leaving Apple. While in 1988 Jobs announced the NeXT Computer from the stage of the Louise M. Davies Symphony Hall across the street, the film would use the San Francisco War Memorial Opera House, shooting from mid-February to mid-March, and saving its neighbor and sister venue, the Davies Symphony Hall, for Act III instead.[5]

Boyle often describes the centerpiece act as a dra-

---

[4] Apple's iconic "1984" commercial directed by Ridley Scott wouldn't make it in full into the finished film, either — the brief clip used onscreen was limited by fair use copyright law after Apple refused to license the commercial, per *The Hollywood Reporter*.

[5] Some of Act II was shot in the real Jobs' former home — Hendrix Dyas said he found the previously unknown address on a blueprint for an early Apple computer in Jobs' famous garage.

matic, Shakespearean story, and the setting reflects that. Hendrix Dyas, the production designer, described the Opera House to *Below the Line* as "the perfect venue for the drama and passion of what is really an act of revenge for Steve, using his new computer almost like a stalking horse to pave his way back to Apple." Art director Peter Borck wrote in *Perspective* that Hendrix Dyas "was looking for a venue that would complement the heightened emotional and narrative intensity of this act while commenting on the theatrical artifice of the product launch." In dramatic gold and red, the Beaux Arts performing space was already dressed the part.

The Opera House, along with the Symphony Hall used in Act III, presented one of the most challenging aspects of shooting the film: operating and scheduling around active performances. "They were shooting during ballet season," John Caldon, communications and events manager for the San Francisco War Memorial & Performing Arts Center, which oversees both venues, told the *Los Angeles Times*, "and it was really complex." Caldon said that on some days, the San Francisco Ballet would be rehearsing onstage while the *Steve Jobs* crew would be shooting elsewhere in the building. On other days, shooting would wait until after ballet performances concluded, usually past 10 p.m., meaning the crew would film from around 11 p.m. through the morning. Cinematographer Alwin H. Küchler describes the short turnover times in production notes: "We would have a drop-dead time to be out of one area, and in a matter of minutes, the space we just evacuated would be full of dancers, musicians, or performers."

Rehearsals helped solidify dialogue and action, but Boyle was determined not to lock the actors into blocking and framing that was so rigid it would limit their performances. "We approached rehearsal and filming in a way that I hoped would liberate the actors physically," Boyle says, "I didn't want the actors to have to worry too much about where they were standing, where they were going." While Sorkin has become known and parodied for the 'walk-and-talk' trope in his work, Boyle saw it as integral to Jobs as a person:

> "The actors are always in motion, through each of these acts. Of course that's partly because these people are in the midst of final preparations for a launch, and there is last-minute business to be taken care of, but it is also very intentional because it was part of Jobs' philosophy. He would walk and talk. He didn't want to sit around having boring meetings. He always wanted to walk and talk because it lent a certain momentum to the undertaking, whatever it may have been."

Küchler and his team worked relentlessly with Boyle to capture "Jobs in perpetual motion." Lighting, framing, focus, rigs, and movement all needed to be able to both follow an overall plan and be responsive to the actors. "We agreed that everything we did had to be about giving priority to the actors and setting the right platform upon which they could function," says the cinematographer.

Steadicam camera stabilizer rigs, operated by Geoff Haley, became a powerful tool in Boyle's arsenal to achieve freedom of movement. Haley, writing in the

Society of Camera Operators publication *Camera Operator*, described conversations with Boyle about plans to shoot the movie like the previous year's *Birdman* — which had simulated the experience of a film made in a single take — and then edit scenes like a traditional movie, allowing actors to have an undisrupted emotional throughline. "Long back-to-back takes racing through the bowels of some of San Francisco's most beautiful architectural landmarks," wrote Haley, "it wasn't unusual to log six miles of carrying my rig in a single day — according to my trusty pedometer."

Problems were solved with collaboration and invisible craft. Many sets had to be photographable in 360 degrees, which meant lighting had to come from practical or hidden sources that wouldn't spoil the illusion of the film. With almost no tape marks to limit the actors' movement, long takes would require some amount of improvisation to capture the scenes. "One of my biggest challenges, in particularly long sequences with complex blocking," wrote Haley,

> "was to remember exactly what I had covered at any given moment in prior takes, because in the next set-up I would need to shoot a different pass of complimentary coverage that would cut well with set-ups I had already shot. Each standalone ten-minute shot needed to contain intercuttable pieces which could be fit together with other passes like a jigsaw puzzle in the editing room."

Graham, the editor, highlights the work of production sound mixer Lisa Pinero capturing sound during filming to allow maximum overlapping of dialogue and minimum use of ADR.[6] He also credits composer Daniel Pemberton with writing temp music that Graham was able to edit to before the composer's score was finalized, and giving the team the chance to verify that Act I was working before beginning Act II. "[Boyle] doesn't care if, say, 10 things are wrong, as long as that one thing is unique, interesting and different," says Graham in production notes. "It felt like the best atmosphere to foster creativity." Haley affirms this feeling in *Camera Operator*: "every once in a while... that rare job comes along, the one that reminds you why you got into the business in the first place, and re-affirms the collaborative power of the medium that we have devoted our lives to."

In 1998, the iMac was launched in the Flint Center and Jobs wore a suit. In 2015, the event was set in the Davies Symphony Hall and Fassbender wore a turtleneck. "It is an instrument unto itself," wrote supervising art director Luke Freeborn in *Perspective*, describing the Symphony Hall "with its fine wood stage and undulating walls, and a prominent feature used to shape the sound, called the cloud, a structure of sixty-five acrylic positionable convex panels suspended directly over the stage and producing a dramatic kaleidoscopic reflection of stage and performer."

Several days of shooting were done in late March, scheduled to not interfere with the San Francisco

---

[6] Short for additional dialogue recording, traditionally part of the post-production process. As an example, ADR is used in Act I to correct a mistake in the script calling Igor Stravinsky's *The Rite of Spring* a symphony.

Symphony. "My gaffer had to rehearse setting up and dismantling lights with a stopwatch," says Küchler, "and he had to continue to practice to get it done in as little time as possible — always faster, faster!" Shooting at night, installing set pieces and decoration right before shooting, and then removing everything at daily wrap, production at times mirrored the attitude Jobs had about the early days at Apple. "It's better to be a pirate than to join the navy," went one of Jobs' maxims from a 1983 Macintosh team retreat, according to Isaacson's biography. Designer Susan Kare, namedropped in the film but never overtly featured in it, clarified in a Stanford University interview, "He meant, 'Let's have a renegade feeling to our group. We can move fast. We can get things done.'"

While Boyle aimed to shoot as much as possible in real spaces, it wasn't always achievable. One quiet part of Act III's production was the use of an 11,000-square-foot set built on a soundstage in Alameda to shoot almost all of the Davies Symphony Hall backstage spaces. Limitations of the performance space pushed the move, but it also allowed the production team to design for the film's needs, such as, per Freeborn, achieving continuous action and angles that wouldn't have been possible at Davies. Backstage spaces customized to the film included Jobs' dressing room — blending the Symphony Hall's convex glass panel features with the Apple aesthetic that influenced 1990s design — and backstage hallway walls covered in Apple ads and 20-foot-tall super-graphics created by graphic designer Emily K. Rolph to bring

Apple's "Think Different" campaign back to life. Blue-grey colors enhanced a design made up of natural woods and glass — here was a hint at the future and Apple's everlasting impact.

In the orchestra pit of the War Memorial Opera House, Wozniak asks Jobs — not a designer, engineer, or guy who uses his hands at all — what it is that he does; Jobs responds, "I play the orchestra." One can imagine a viewer asking any film director the same question and getting much the same answer. "An orchestra does not pick up their instruments and perform a perfect *Ninth Symphony* right out of the gate," Daniels says in the production notes. Time, details, behind-the-scenes planning all builds to the finished product — as with a product launch, when it comes to movies, the public usually only sees the polished, finished work.

"The hope was that the film would accumulate into something bigger than the sum of its parts, which is a portrait of a guy's mind and what's involved in forging something new, the sacrifices that are made, and how you can't really achieve full success," Boyle told *Interview Magazine*. Whatever the results, critically, financially, or culturally, the *Steve Jobs* team created something with a consistent message from all of those involved in making it: it was an effort of many minds and talents, drawn together by teamwork, unified to achieve a single goal, a sometimes impossible mission. Invisible as it may be, un-newsworthy as it may seem, that collaboration did produce something bigger than the sum of its parts. And now, it is acknowledged.

Jobs

by Aashima Rawal

Backstage at the Flint Center for the Performing Arts in 1984, everything feels unsettled — wires snake across the floor, techs fiddle with equipment, and onstage, a few people argue about what might go wrong. *Steve Jobs* starts here — not in the legend of the garage, not in the neatness of a boardroom, but in the in-between space where nerves and possibility collide. Aaron Sorkin's script gives the dialogue its edge, but Suttirat Larlarb's costumes do something quieter: they sketch the character as he speaks. Across the film's three acts, the legendary subject Steve Jobs shifts — first restless, then measured, then iconic. The black mock turtleneck lands in the final act not as a flourish, but as the closing line of a sentence you've been reading the whole time.

His first outfit barely registers. A shirt, some trousers — ordinary, maybe forgettable. He puts on a bowtie, and it looks kind of dated. But as the story unfolds, the clothing starts to say more. It shows how identity, especially the public kind, can be made as carefully as any product design. And that idea isn't limited to Apple. In India, where Jobs spent time early in life seeking spirituality, cloth has always carried messages. Khadi, with its uneven hand-spun weave, and kantha, with its rows of stitches building layer upon layer, both turn fabric into declaration. In *Steve Jobs*, clothes aren't just what you wear — they hold memory, they signal intention, they last.

In the years since Jobs' passing, tech demos have proliferated, imitating the Apple icon's product launch presentations (the devoted called them "Stevenotes"), full of impressive numbers, grand statements, and dramatic reveals. Jobs wasn't born a keynote magician. In the late 1970s, he often stumbled, struggling to translate what he already saw in his head into something a crowd could follow. To most people, "personal computer" sounded like science fiction. He was pitching not just hardware but a leap of imagination. The belief was there — palpable — but the delivery was rough around the edges.

That changed at the 1984 Macintosh launch. The Mac spoke in its own synthesized voice; the crowd roared. Engineer Andy Hertzfeld, documenting the history of the computer in his book *Revolution in the Valley*, described the response: "Pandemonium reigned." The triumph wasn't only the machine — it was the way Jobs framed it. He had established a formula: treat the product launch like a story with setup, tension, and release. The stage became another canvas to design.

His years in exile at NeXT pushed this further. In 1988 at the Louise M. Davies Symphony Hall in San Francisco, Jobs staged something closer to a premiere than a tech demo — spotlights, pacing, slides timed like music cues. Colleagues remembered rehearsals so obsessive that every gesture and transition was practiced until they looked effortless. It was a craft precisely honed through repetition.

By his return to Apple in 1997, the performance had hardened into doctrine. Keynotes turned into cultural events, replayed on TV and dissected like pop concerts. Jobs rehearsed them line by line, gesture by gesture, until the margin of error shrank to nothing. The 2007 iPhone reveal at the Macworld trade show (beyond the film's timeframe but essential to the persona onscreen) distilled it all in one sly trick: promise three revolutionary tech products, then unveil them as just one device. It was narrative sleight of hand executed with a designer's precision.

Steve Jobs is structured around three pressure-cooker acts: 1984 (Macintosh), 1988 (NeXT), and 1998 (iMac). All of them unfold backstage and around their respective venues, in the charged minutes before Jobs steps into the spotlight. Within that narrow frame, the smallest details take on unusual weight. Costumes, in particular, become a kind of silent dialogue. Jobs' iconic mock turtleneck doesn't appear until the third act — a crucial act of patience.

The movie opens with 30 minutes to curtain. Michael Fassbender's Jobs stares at an error screen in the Macintosh demo, barking his instructions. He's dressed in a pressed shirt and tailored trousers — polished, slightly conservative, the look of someone trying to be taken seriously. The suit's colors lean dark, but they stop short of the severe palette we'll see later. The outfit breathes. It hints at drive and talent, but not myth. "I've had a chance to make a lot of mistakes," Jobs once told then-journalist Michael Moritz in an interview. "Your aesthetics get better as you make mistakes."

Fassbender's costume — which evokes but does not totally mimic the real Jobs' outfit at the momentous 1984 keynote — evolves over the course of Act I. He notices that the demo disk fits in an engineer's pocket and, amid attempting to reshape the universe, he reshapes his wardrobe, demanding a shirt with a breast pocket. Jobs is a man of precision: "the Mac is beige, I'm beige, the disk is blue; the shirt has to be white."

When Jobs walks back into his dressing room in his undershirt, there is a gesture of precision as he tucks it in — the man cannot abide imprecision — but moments later, in a double-breasted suit and striped green bowtie, he is far from a streamlined product. The Macintosh was revolutionary, but Jobs himself was still a young founder learning how to present. Larlarb, who began working with Boyle on *Sunshine*, described the 1984 costume in a *Film Doctor* interview as being designed for "someone who suddenly gets a lot of money and can afford [a suit] but it's not quite him yet." The tension shows in the fit and the movement — clothes that look neat but restless, mirroring a man still working out who he is in public.

By the NeXT Computer launch in 1988, the atmosphere feels noticeably different, and the costumes underline that shift. Fassbender's Jobs has shed the looser shirts and trousers of 1984. In their place are sharply tailored jackets with defined shoulders, trousers pressed into clean lines, and an overall silhouette that feels more deliberate and controlled. The fabrics seem weightier — wool or wool blends that drape with intention, a marked change from the softer cottons of the first act.

Even the palette evolves. Muted tones give way to deep charcoal, navy, and other commanding shades that suggest authority without pushing into the stark black he'll eventually adopt. His outline looks deliberate, almost armored, shaped to project control. Larlarb described looking at pictures of Jobs from the era: "He looks like he has ambition but he also looks like he's trying to figure out how to play the game a bit." In this second act of the film and his career, the costumes suggest someone experimenting with power dressing — disciplined, strategic, but still unfinished.

In Act III, the iMac is about to reframe what a computer looks like: translucent shell, bright colors, hardware that invites users to display it like a piece of modern art rather than hide it under a desk. Against that burst of playfulness, Jobs enters in stark contrast — black mock turtleneck, Levi's 501s, and New Balance sneakers. You know the look — it's etched into cultural memory.

Jobs wasn't wearing the look in 1998, but the movie needs it to complete the arc. This is costume as payoff, a uniform donned by a legend at the height of this power. When it appears, it doesn't just dress the character — it completes him.

Why a uniform at all? For Jobs, clothing was never an afterthought. It was part of the system he built around himself. He saw simplicity not as a style but as a working rule, the same way he treated design. Clarity, in his view, was a form of respect. And respect began with attention — something he considered the rarest currency in both design and life. If attention was limited, then even small choices, like what to wear in the morning, had to be managed carefully.

The story of the turtleneck's origin has been retold many times (including in the film's source text, Walter Isaacson's biography *Steve Jobs*), but it's worth pausing over. In the 1980s, Jobs visited Sony's factories in Japan and noticed that employees wore uniforms designed by Issey Miyake. The effect stayed with him: a workforce moving as one, immediately recognizable as part of a shared purpose. Apple wasn't interested in adopting the idea for staff, but Jobs carried it home for himself. He looked to Miyake to be the source of a personal uniform and ordered stacks of identical black mock turtlenecks created by the pioneering designer. It wasn't a fashion statement so much as an operating choice. One decision removed. One fewer trivial distraction before getting to the work that mattered.

The same principle ran through Apple's products. The iPod didn't win because it had a longer list of features. It won because its capacitive sensing click wheel made the experience of listening to music almost effortless. The iPhone stunned people not by cramming in more buttons but by removing them, leaving a smooth pane of glass that could shift into whatever the user needed. Even Apple Stores worked this way: wide sightlines, uncluttered tables, bright light. The design nudged your focus straight to the devices. Apple's ads followed the same rhythm: a short phrase, one striking image, plenty of white space.

Jobs' version of simplicity was never cold. He wasn't stripping things away to leave emptiness; he was stripping them back to reveal feeling. He wanted the first encounter — the moment your hand touched the prod- uct — to feel natural, as if the design had already antici- pated you. His uniform mirrored that conviction. Day after day, the same outline: steady, deliberate, distrac- tion-free.

The other key was consistency. A single outfit, repeated across years, becomes a kind of shorthand. It verifies identity on sight the way a logo does. What began as a practical trick soon hardened into a symbol. By the late 1990s, the black turtleneck wasn't just what Jobs wore — it was what he stood for. Focus, discipline, continuity. Not subtraction for its own sake but paring back until only the essential remained visible.

If you want to see fabric act like language, look to India. During the 20th century independence movement, Mahatma Gandhi and other leaders championed the hand-spun cloth khadi as a symbol of independence from foreign textile manufacturers. Run your fingers across the rough cotton and you feel the unevenness, the slow rhythm of a wheel turned by hand. To wear it was to take a side: against imported cloth, for local labor, for self-reliance. Its rough edges weren't flaws — they were evidence. Every thread said: this was made by someone's hands, not by a machine.

Kantha, from the Bengal region of India, speaks differently. A centuries-old practice of repurposing fabric for practical uses, kantha was more than just conservation. Women would take old saris and scraps, layering them into quilts held together with a running stitch. Each patch carried its own history: one may have wrapped a bride, another may have cradled a child. The repeated stitch gave the fabric a pulse — quiet, steady, like breathing. When you look closely, you don't just see cloth; you see lives stacked together.

Khadi pares things down. Kantha layers them up.

One is refusal, the other remembrance. Both prove that clothing can be more than fabric against skin. It can hold memory, mark history, and tell stories without words. Khadi turned its back on mass production, insisting on being slow, handmade, and rooted in human effort. Jobs, in his own way, refused to play by fashion's churn. He kept to one outline, season after season. Both choices were deliberate and a little defiant: one against colonial imports, the other against corporate polish.

A black turtleneck on its own is neutral, even forgettable. But repeat it — on stage after stage, in photo after photo — and it begins to gather weight. Over years, an article of clothing turns into a signal; the repetition makes meaning. Kantha quilts work in the same way. Scraps of cloth, each with its own past life, are layered and stitched until they form a coherent whole. What once was leftover becomes a memory you can touch. Jobs' uniform followed a similar arc: every launch, every keynote added another layer to its significance until the outfit became shorthand for his way of working.

It's easy to label all this 'minimalism,' but that misses the point. Khadi isn't about being bare; it's about showing the hands that spun it. Kantha isn't about clean lines; it's about what is saved and stitched back together. And Jobs wasn't trying to erase himself with a simple outfit. He was protecting his focus, reserving his energy for choices that mattered. What unites them is not austerity but intent: pick a form, honor it, and let it deepen over time.

There's also the matter of legibility. Khadi carries its

process in its uneven weave. Kantha leaves visible traces of past lives — wedding cloth, baby blankets, old saris reborn as quilts. Jobs' silhouette, thrown against the light of a projector screen, was instantly recognizable, even in outline. In each case, the meaning doesn't need to be explained. It sits on the surface, ready to be read.

The black turtleneck was never an act of denial. These were good-quality pieces — Miyake made them durable, designed to survive years of use. Jobs simply wanted less clutter in his day. The aim was focus. As the outline stayed steady, what came forward was Jobs' voice, his pacing, his intensity. The clothes faded into the background so the man could step into view. It was the details that mattered: when to pause, how to frame a product, how to stage the reveal. The repetition of his outfit cleared the deck for variation elsewhere.

The uniform was a tool, a kind of filter. It conserved Jobs' attention and turned consistency into a statement. In a culture that prizes novelty, consistency looked like authority. Seen next to khadi and kantha, the picture sharpens. Khadi wove politics into its threads. Kantha stitched memory into scraps. Jobs embedded the method into his own outline. Each shows that material, treated with intent and persistence, can speak louder than words.

In *Steve Jobs*, a story of dressing rooms and backstage hallways, we can see the pressure of image-making —

Apple co-founder Steve Wozniak even criticizes Jobs for his artificiality: "I'm the only one who knows that this guy here is someone you invented." We see the kind of image-making that happens in tight spaces, just before the lights come up. In those narrow corridors, there's no room for sweeping biography or long exposition. Every detail has to carry weight: a pause, a glance, the way a shirt falls on the shoulder.

Apple's devices carried the same instinct and intention as Jobs' wardrobe. Buttons disappeared, gestures became smoother, screens grew cleaner. The point wasn't absence for its own sake; it was to leave room for people to focus on what they wanted to do. In the film and in reality, after seeing Jobs build his identity through error after error and trial, his uniform is something of a conclusion to a line that was building ever since the garage. The clothes don't decorate Jobs — they name him.

That's why the black turtleneck lingers — not as a fashion quirk, but as a method. Whether under stage lights in California or in a courtyard in Bengal, the lesson feels similar: choose deliberately, repeat with care, and let meaning gather with time.

Sorkin

By Kat Trout-Baron

In "Notes on the Auteur Theory in 1962," Andrew Sarris outlines three distinct qualities of the director that prove their ownership over a cinematic work: a director must be technologically competent, stylistically distinct, and in possession of a rich interior. As an example, the film critic describes a moment in *The Rules of the Game* where director and actor Jean Renoir charges up the stairs, pauses, and continues his ascent. The moment of hesitation is perceived as graceful and intimate, proof of a director's personality within the final cut. Technology intervenes in the cinematic process — footage is fed through machines, compressed or stretched until it can be shown theatrically. Sarris' auteurs (coming from the French term for authors) survive such technological manipulation, remaining present within the project. Concern with auteurism stems from its dismissal of other bodies present in the cinematic process. Various roles are omitted — editors, producers, and most glaringly, screenwriters.

A film does not exist until ink is spilled, characters and setting fleshed out on the page. Aaron Sorkin's script for *Steve Jobs,* later directed by Danny Boyle, has various Sorkinisms — quirks associated with him rather than the director. Sarris describes Renoir's moments of hesitation as bursts of personality, the voice of a craftsman undeniable. Sorkin's scripts have similar flourishes of individualism, namely in pauses between intense lines that render the film immobile. There's a poignant scene in Act III where Steve Jobs argues about the payment of his daughter's tuition with his old colleague Andy Hertzfeld. Hertzfeld's line, "she needed things, she needed socks," is followed on the page by a written beat. Unsaid words exist within that beat, more profound because of their absence. Later in their conversation, Hertzfeld asks Jobs why he is adamant about being hated. Jobs responds, "I'm indifferent to whether they dislike me," which prompts his former chief engineer to reply "I always have." Jobs responds with a witty rebuttal, but first pauses, suggesting the emotional impact of Hertzfeld's words. In that beat, Sorkin subtly directs performance — it is a cue to react, the conversation coming to its crushing end.

For a character like Jobs, Sorkin's beats are evidence of his caginess — the truth exists within these standstills. His shortcomings as a father, friend, and person are left within the moments he cannot instantly mask hurt. Another instance occurs in Jobs' final argument with his daughter, Lisa, the culmination of their tension surrounding familial legitimacy. Jobs insists he always meant to pay for tuition, which prompts Lisa to bring up his rejection of her as a daughter. In her fury, Lisa dismisses the iMac, calling it "Judy Jetson's Easy-Bake Oven" and pointing out the grammatical errors in its slogan, Think Different. After her diss, Jobs once again pauses, then says (in a moment that doesn't make the final film), "There is no way in the world that's not my kid." Once again, the hesitation represents a moment where Sorkin sculpts performance. The insults, which previously moved Jobs into temperamental silence, are presented as impressive. Jobs sees himself. The through-line of Sorkin's script is Jobs' relationship with his daughter — the beat helps maintain suspense, eventually delivering closure. Like Renoir's hesitation at the top of the stairs, Sorkin's pause suggests an auteurist personality. An analysis of the *Steve Jobs* shooting script makes evident Sorkin's technical fluency, individual style, and interiority.

Steve Jobs is written with awareness of the camera; Sorkin includes transitions and edits within scenic descriptions, curating the movement of the film. Most prominently, Sorkin utilizes the em dash — represented on the page as "--" — to establish location and shot changes. The first sentence of the *Steve Jobs* screenplay starts with the em dash: "--we're in the middle of a confidential conversation." The first line of a script establishes the tone of the piece, as well as the intent of the author. It is the first impression of a project, a series of words that decides if an audience will remain. Sorkin bypasses a lengthy or descriptive line, instead dropping his audience into an active scene. The em dash implies previous movement; the scene occurring is not the beginning of the story. The viewer is eavesdropping, witnessing private moments happening with or without them. From this em dash, the director, audience, and crew learn the pace of the film. Furthermore, while bare in elaborate detail, the first line solidifies location. It guides the director and crew — three people (Joanna Hoffman, Hertzfeld, and Jobs) having a private conversation limits the possibilities of the space. Throughout the script, Sorkin uses the em dash as a way to communicate cuts and scenic transitions. On page five, when introducing a secondary character, Sorkin writes, "Andrea Cunningham, a 26-year-old publicist for Apple, calls from the back--". The em dash acts as a cut — the next line in the script is Cunningham's, implying a shot of her within the film. It is a cue to move away and open the film up from the whisperings of the three, now utilizing more space. Such a technique is implemented consistently; it appears again on page 25, when Chrisann Brennan, Jobs' ex-lover, confronts him backstage. In the description, Brennan "points to the Mac that's sitting on a table--". After this visual, Brennan's line is "So that's it?" Once again, the em dash expresses a shift in focus. It directs the scene, asking for the audience to follow the Macintosh instead of Brennan and Jobs.

In transitions between locations, Sorkin's em dash assists in maintaining time. *Steve Jobs* is written in three acts, each part limited to a specific year. Moreso, within those distinct years, each act occurs during one day. To remain tight and focused, Sorkin moves characters through one primary location in each act. The slug lines (location indicators identified in a script by INT/EXT) are accompanied by the word "continuous," suggesting that time has not passed. The em dash assists this direction, further infusing the script with fluidity. The movement between scenes is written as such: "STEVE steps out into-- / INT. HALLWAY - CONTINUOUS / --where ANDY HERTZ-FELD is waiting..." In the final cut, Sorkin's descriptions command movement of the camera, maintaining continuity from room to room. A shot will show Jobs and company exiting a space, then cut to them on the other side. Sometimes, it will follow them through rooms, allowing characters to walk and talk. The em dash connects the scenic descriptions, maintaining cohesion within prose. The words are kinetic, characters remaining in motion from page to page. Moreso, its built-in suggestions for camera movement suggest Sorkin's comprehension of cinematic techniques. Sorkin's script is a living, breathing body — it does not read as a suggestion of what *could* happen on screen, but an explicit document of what *will* happen.

Sorkin's voice is not buried in the translation from script to screen; in fact, when involved, many characteristics of the film can be associated with Sorkin. A common rule in screenwriting denotes that one page will equal one minute of screentime. Sorkin's scripts defy such logic — *Steve Jobs'* is 189 pages, but the runtime is 122 minutes. And while some scenes or moments don't make the final cut, most of the material remains, condensed at a breakneck speed. One tool behind Sorkin's speed is the parenthetical, which is often used to indicate a line reading. Sorkin's parenthetical primarily serves as an interrupting force. Lines will include the following direction: (over); this suggests lines that begin before the preceding ones end, resulting in feverish, overlapping, impatient conversation. The effectiveness of such a choice can be felt during Jobs' argument with his partner Steve Wozniak before the launch of the Macintosh. The Apple co-founders' argument spans 10 pages — the first half is a back and forth with no interruptions. Near the climax, (over) appears before nearly every line; Jobs lets the truth slip and (over) controls the momentum of the fight.

```
                    WOZ
          Do you concede that the slots (are
          the reason for the success of)--


                   STEVE
              (over)
          We can't possibly still be talking
          about the slots, man, it's been
          seven years and--


                    WOZ
          I have a point. The eight slots on
          (the Apple II are what)--


                   STEVE
              (over)
          You're still doing it, you're
          talking about the slots, there's
          something wrong (with you).
```

```
          WOZ
     (over)
  The slots--


          STEVE
  This argument started in the
  garage!
```

As evident above, parentheses also denote which lines should be interrupted. Sorkin's (over) serves as the trigger, nudging an actor to press down. Words buried beneath interruptions are often the most salacious details, blunt truths, and frustrated jabs. The execution mimics a natural argument — quick and impossible, no person given complete control. Sorkin's command appears throughout the script, nudging a scene along — lines run parallel, no single person meant to possess the spotlight.

In other Sorkin scripts, parentheticals also control the timing of dialogue; (beat) appears consistently in *The Social Network*, communicating the calculation necessary from each character. Mark Zuckerberg is on trial, defending his choices despite how malicious they seem on paper. In *Steve Jobs*, (over) denotes spur-of-the-moment emotions. In *The Social Network*, (beat) showcases the aftermath, tense characters planning their attack. While *Steve Jobs* quickens dialogue and *Social Network* slows it down, both parentheticals are displays of Sorkin's ability to control time on the page. Beyond technique, the dialogue also serves as an indication of Sorkin's unique perspective. A common feature found in Sorkin's scripts are lengthy, drawn-out insults, often aided by vivid imagery. In Sorkin's first screenplay, *A Few Good Men*, Lieutenant (junior grade) Daniel Kaffee stumbles home drunk after a blow in a case defending two marines. Dismayed, he lashes out at his co-counsel, perplexed by their positive outlook:

```
                    KAFFEE
        Yes. No problem. We get it from him.
           (to SAM)
        Colonel, isn't it true that you
        ordered the Code Red on Santiago?


                     SAM
        Look, we're all a little --


                    KAFFEE
        I'm sorry, your time's run out. What
        do we have for the losers, Judge?
        Well, for our defendants it's a
        lifetime at exotic Fort Levenworth.
        [sic]
        And for defense counsel Kaffee? That's
        right -- it's -- a court -- martial.
        Yes, Johnny, after falsely accusing
        a marine officer of conspiracy, Lt.
        Kaffee will have a long and prosperous
        career teaching typewriter maintenance
        at the Rocco Columbo School for Women.
        Thank you for playing "Should We or
        Should-We-Not Follow the Advice of
        the Galacticly [sic] Stupid".
```

Spoken as a drunken, elaborately concocted game show monologue, Kaffee's rant is directed at Lieutenant Commander Jo Galloway and decorated with Sorkin's signature, hyper-specific scenarios; the prize of "teaching typewriter maintenance at the Rocco Columbo School for Women" stands in for demotion and the end of

Kaffee's military career. It is an elaborate way of emasculating himself and digging at Jo's femininity. Sorkin's barbs are quotable, wordy, and convoluted — Kaffee's intent is to call Jo stupid and overzealous; it takes him half a page to say what he means. In a similar, pivotal scene in *The Social Network*, Eduardo Saverin storms through Facebook headquarters, aghast at the news he's being edged out of the company he helped start. Saverin charges toward Mark Zuckerberg's desk and smashes his laptop; Sean Parker, who has wedged himself between the two friends, interrupts Saverin's confrontation — Eduardo turns to him:

```
                    EDUARDO
          Sorry, but my Prada's at the cleaners
          along with my hoodie and my fuck-you
          flip-flops you pretentious douchebag.
```

Like Kaffee's long-winded rant, Saverin's comment has the intent to maim. It is also primarily made of references, an expansive scene with an inevitable punch. Kaffee describes a game show, Saverin an order at the laundromat. Both jabs are snappy, repeatable, and hurtful.

Sorkin's *Steve Jobs* script includes its own extravagant disses; during a poignant spat, Wozniak likens his and Jobs' positions within Apple to those of The Beatles: "I don't like talking like this but I am tired of being Ringo when I know I was John." The following quarrel unfolds:

<pre>
                    STEVE
          Everybody loves Ringo!

                    WOZ
          And I'm tired of being patronized
          by you.

                    STEVE
          You think John became John by
          winning a raffle, Woz? You think he
          tricked somebody or hit George
          Harrison over the head? He was John
          because he was John.

                    WOZ
          He was John because he wrote
          "Ticket to Ride" and I wrote the
          Apple II.
</pre>

Once again, Sorkin's references stand in for a bitter truth. John Lennon and Ringo Starr were part of the same band, but they achieved separate levels of fame; Woz and John are aware the same has occurred within Apple. Woz and Jobs each want to be John, the leader of the band — they want credit for what they have created.

Situating a screenwriter's interiority is difficult; Sarris' auteur theory focuses on visual cues, insisting depth belongs in what is seen. There is no regard for what flourishes may belong to other creatives, embedded within the image. Sarris' example of interiority is Renoir's *The Rules of the Game* and the lingering staircase. By hanging in that moment, Renoir pushes the film further. He is more curious about what film can do to communicate character than he is interested in making something fitting cinematic standards. A screenwriter's interiority cannot be perceived from the final cut; to discover their deeper meaning, a viewer must consult the script. Bits of the writer are found within lengthy descriptions, notes to actors explaining the emotions of their character. Throughout *Steve Jobs,* Sorkin includes asides that pause movement on the page, comments meant for a reader and not a viewer. They include subjective details, hinting at Sorkin's opinions on his characters. When a character is introduced in a script, a writer often includes a short, encompassing description. In his description of Wozniak, Sorkin writes, "STEVE (WOZ) WOZNIAK sticks his head in the door. WOZ is amiable. He's not looking for trouble and while he's an undisputed genius, he doesn't have Steve's anger or Steve's polish." Sorkin bypasses typical script details such as age and physique, instead focusing on a judgment of character. He does not use the word "amiable" as a compliment — it is a flaw, the trait that separates Wozniak from Jobs. It continues in his next sentence, where Sorkin admits Wozniak is a genius, but lacks aspects of Jobs' personality. The writer makes evident his perspective on success: there are certain factors that create stars and snuff them. It is less of a character description and more of a rumination, othering Wozniak. Such commentary can be found in other descriptions — during Jobs' final conversation with John Sculley, his father-figure-turned-backstabber, Sorkin provides a lengthy account of their positions:

```
There's a moment of shock as STEVE and
SCULLEY take in the sight of each other.
```

```
Sculley's always been a handsome man--a
healthy, well-scrubbed, Connecticut guy--
but he was sent to Florida much too
young. And he's been living a secluded
life as the guy who traded Babe Ruth.
STEVE can see that.
```

Like Wozniak, Sculley's character is dissected in relation to Jobs. Wozniak and Sculley are placed on the wrong side of history, not as recognizable as Jobs, and Sorkin provides a blunt explanation. As a leader, Wozniak lacked anger or polish. As a manager, Sculley did not maintain star power. Once again, Sorkin's descriptions hint at his feelings regarding talent and legacy; to stay, a person must be formidable. As a script-writer, Sorkin has acquired an abnormal amount of attention; it is a position usually overlooked and under-valued. Sorkin's voice and celebrity have provided him more freedom on the page, as well as an identity separate from his director's. Sorkin has no reason to be insecure — neither did Jobs. Each is aware of his oeuvre and its personal and social consequences. Sorkin's interiority appears in his judgment of character, suggesting a relation to Job's celebrity and the self-importance required to last.

Sorkin is living proof: a screenwriter can be cognizant of mechanical techniques, style, and personality, sharpening their craft to remain prominent throughout a film's life. A director may be behind the camera, shaping a picture on set, but a film begins with its writer. Sorkin, who guides a picture from its title page, maintains authorship and auteurship.

Boyle

by Scout Tafoya

There is, in the cinema of Danny Boyle, a rough attempt to survey the United Kingdom's complete economic and aesthetic history. The skeleton key is his opening ceremony for the 2012 Olympic Games. This director, who had taken great pains to be associated with yuppie derangement, heroin addicts, zombies, poor kids, strivers, dreamers, nobodies... Here he was paying tribute, in the largest venue he'd ever been guaranteed, the eyes of the world watching him, to the industrial progress of the United Kingdom. Mark Renton, the wiry dead-ender hero of 1996's *Trainspotting*'s always timely screed was that "It's SHITE being Scottish!

> "We're the lowest of the low. The scum of the fucking Earth! The most wretched, miserable, servile, pathetic trash that was ever shat into civilization. Some people hate the English. I don't. They're just wankers. We, on the other hand, are colonized by wankers! Can't even find a decent culture to be colonized by."

And it was met by a churning, yearning dance of steel mill

workers, suffragettes, landlords, poets, all led by a top-hatted Kenneth Branagh quoting Shakespeare in the guise of a historic British engineer while wage slaves toiled away elsewhere. It was a vulgar display of nationalist fervor. It seemed to betray Boyle's interest in the lower classes and communal life; from the clique of heroin addicts and artists in *Strumpet*, *Trainspotting*, and *Pistol* to the gaggle of urchins in *Millions* to the socialist camps in *The Beach* and *28 Years Later*. Boyle seemed interested in people perpetually looking at the stars from the gutter, until for a moment he couldn't help train his camera on the privileged. And yet it wasn't so simple, because, it turns out, he was playing a longer, stranger game: England as a suit of clothes. The cinema as church worshipping false gods. He was complicit in the deconstruction of his own project. The sight of dancers and drummers dressed in 19th century rags swaying and dancing for a crowd of onlookers was an unforced error of spectacle. England really did make the poor dance to their tune. Did Boyle know it?

If we accept Boyle's role as a producer and director of TV movies in the '80s and '90s as the first phase of his career, his move to theatrical features as his second, and the Olympics as the start of a new, valedictory phase, it's the central question of this third phase of the English director's career. Boyle made the leap from pop counter-culture provocateur to England's prosaic novelist laureate when he was asked to represent the English character as distinct nationally from everywhere else, and suddenly the bulk of his work shifted into place. Just why was it that all of his movies are about people trying to get rich? To find paradise? To be among the ruling class? *Shallow Grave*'s trio of nobodies set against each other for a pile of cash, *Trainspotting*'s heroin addicts see a robbery as their ticket out of trap houses, the couple in *A Life Less Ordinary* commit a series of real crimes for money they don't even need, the boys of *Millions* learn they can't keep stolen money even when it drops in from heaven, and well, *Slumdog Millionaire*. There is thus a series of images of doubt in the mission all through his filmography: money and rapaciousness are the undoing of the heroes of *The Beach, Millions, Trance, Yesterday,* and *Pistol*. Perfection and paradise, ever out of reach because you can't have everything and nothing at once.

Complicating things further is that Boyle was one of the first people to start popularizing a democratizing technological tool: the Mini-DV digital camera. Suddenly all one needed to make a movie was a camera no bigger than a football. The first major digitally shot films, Thomas Vinterberg's *Festen* or *The Celebration* and Lars Von Trier's *The Idiots*, the flagship films of the Danish Dogme 95 movement both competed at the 1998 Cannes Film Festival. Though neither won the Palme d'Or (*The Celebration* walked off with the Jury Prize), they were the films that changed cinema forever. Boyle hired *Festen*'s cinematographer, English-born Anthony Dod Mantle, and quickly made a pair of films about capitalism and art. In *Strumpet*, a homeless derelict becomes a pop star with the help of her just about destitute, John Cooper Clarke–styled poet friend. In *Vacuuming Completely Nude in*

Paradise, Timothy Spall plays a grotesque door-to-door salesman who slowly loses his livelihood as the internet renders him obsolete. Both wrestle with what technology makes possible and whether happiness and lucre must cancel each other out. Both have utopian images in the finale, with an ecstatic *Top of the Pops* performance giving the *Strumpet* strivers a glimpse of paradise on their own terms, and with a group of vacuum salesman performing a joyless Busby Berkeley pantomime dance number to Sheena Easton's "Morning Train (Nine to Five)." You really only believe one of them.

When Boyle helped popularize the digital camera (*28 Days Later...*, his and Dod Mantle's debut theatrical collaboration, made over nine times its 8 million dollar budget back), he was metamorphosing cinema into something else. The gatekeeping was over, the lengthy post-production process was shrunk, and soon the Sundance Film Festival was full of micro-budget, digitally shot movies. By the end of the decade, directors as disparate as Steven Soderbergh, David Lynch, Michael Mann, Michael Winterbottom, George Lucas, and Francis Ford Coppola had all experimented with digital cameras on expensive or expansive canvases. Boyle never looked back, allowing the range of motion and placement digital cameras afforded him to hone his form and focus his aesthetics. With digital, the color of a room or a space could change more easily — the camera came with a built-in monitor. Every change to lighting is registered immediately, and, in the edit, the color of a single image can be manipulated instantaneously. Boyle was suddenly quoting

Van Gogh's *Tournesols* every chance he got, with brilliant sunflowers overwhelming the frames, each time producing a cathedral of color, an image that appeared to have been captured through stained glass rather than a camera lens (find the flowers in his pilot for the F/X miniseries *Trust*, in *Trance, T2 Trainspotting, 28 Days Later...*, and its sequel). It was as if by turning to the paintings of a starving artist for inspiration he could complicate his turn toward the mainstream. Furthermore, in investigating England from the birth of the Industrial Age (*Mr. Wroe's Virgins*, his Olympics ceremony *Isles of Wonder*, his adaptation of *Frankenstein* for a canted stage) through to its return to preindustrial feudalism (*28 Years Later*), he was linking cinema to the analog arts through digital investigation, returning to an age before Thomas Hardy's writing about the empire's localized failings. Turning a camera into a paintbrush, a piece of colored glass. Like Michael Winterbottom, Boyle seemed interested in Hardy's vision of England as a place of immovable class distinctions and inexorable degradation (even *Sunshine*'s obsession with the sun recalls the pre-modern paganism that held England in its grip before the introduction of Roman Catholicism to the country in the 7th century). Unlike Winterbottom, Boyle doesn't believe in unhappy endings. Someone's always smiling when his movies end, even if there's no reason to smile.

Steve Jobs centers on product launches, taking the form of highly theatrical backstage dramas. Alternating between the melancholy carnivalesque of Federico Fellini & Alberto Lattuada's *Variety Lights,* the self-seriousness of

Alejandro González Iñárritu's *Birdman,* and the comic neuroses of Peter Bogdanovich's *Noises Off,* we see Apple visionary Steve Jobs unable to focus on giving the spiffiest presentation he can. Everyone in his orbit chooses the half hour before curtain to air their grievances and, though he talks a big game about needing to focus, one senses that Jobs thrives on the conflict and lives for the shouting matches. His people, like the ghosts and memories of Charles Dickens' *A Christmas Carol,* represent who he might have been in another life — a rumpled programmer, a concerned father, a calculating banker, someone's subordinate — without his X factor: vision.

Boyle meanwhile makes a case for his own vision by orchestrating the madness around his hero/antihero. Given a typically verbose Aaron Sorkin script filled with tech jargon, cultural references, and catalogs of very real slights, Boyle places Jobs under harsh and heavy lights and spins around him as if taking up the spaces in which his thoughts materialize. If Boyle's camera and edit don't always think *with* Jobs, they toggle between the speed of thought and the sweatiness of his attempts to shirk his responsibilities to other people. His old allies and friends and the mother of his daughter all appear as if as surprise witnesses in court. He can't help but fight tooth and nail for a purity of vision in which, at last, no one is caught in his whirlwind after so much arguing and friction, both as a protective reflex of them and himself and the spitting frustration in which it manifests. The film grows more ingratiating further into that whirlwind, with Jobs struggling hard to eject doubt from his thoughts before placing himself before the comparatively benign judgment of the public. Bad press affects him, churning that water and darkening the skies, even if we're always under cinematographer Alwin H. Küchler's overpowering lighting design. He places what would otherwise be a rich color scheme in aggressive harmony with Jobs' mood swings. The buzzing lights of horrible 1980s dressing rooms and the clinically anodyne conference rooms of the 1990s become deeply uncomfortable places because Jobs is in them. With its leapfrog montage and lightning repartee, the film gives the impression of a more dizzying form than it actually displays. As in the shower scene in *Psycho* or the kitchens and dining rooms of *The Texas Chain Saw Massacre,* the piece suggests that we've seen more violence than we have. There is, however, no lack of psychological wounds.

Boyle's self-reflexivity and doubts find their apotheosis in *Steve Jobs,* which begins (after a brief prologue featuring author Arthur C. Clarke) with an image of an empty auditorium, suggesting, of course, an empty movie theater. Jobs helped give everyone a camera on their phones, implicitly turning everyone into a filmmaker. *Steve Jobs* starts by asking, also implicitly, if audiences will gather with the ease and comfort of technology at home. Will there be anyone left to partake of cinema when we are all directors? The film is a nimble work of synaptic thinking and heavy-handed demonstration, of images and text on the screen to showcase what the cinematic image becomes in the 21st century from the vantage point of the birth of the digital camera. While the Welsh filmmaker Peter

Greenaway's years of bad reviews turned him into a niche figure, Boyle's similarly overstuffed cinema made him an Oscar-winning populist, the Queen of England's personal filmmaker — for whom else would she pretend to skydive into Olympic Stadium? Even if he turned down a knighthood, he was still offered one.

Greenaway tried to turn cinema into an art that incorporated all other arts — opera, architecture, sculpture, gallery installations, classical music, pop music, painting, calligraphy, tattoo — and in so doing presented a vision of the cinema at once singular and too highbrow to survive the transition to digital. When the cinema lost its footing as the popular art form, it became the province of hobbyists empowered by the digital age Boyle had helped usher in. "When Dylan wrote 'Shelter from the Storm' he didn't ask people to contribute to the lyrics," argues Jobs when told to make his computer more accessible. Greenaway looked to masters of art — Shakespeare, Rembrandt, Brecht, Étienne-Louis Boullée — to give the cinema the discipline of classicism. Boyle tried to make vulgar populist concerns — Bollywood dance numbers, zombie movies, cell phones, The Beatles, vacuums — into the stuff of classical art (Goya and Rembrandt make appearances in *The Nightwatch* and *Trance*), and their creators and salesmen into figures akin to religious icons. "Computers aren't paintings," says Steve Wozniak, Apple's lead programmer. And Boyle fills his screen with projected words, Skylab launching into space, Ridley Scott's "1984" Apple computer commercial, scenes of an audience doing the wave silently, as if in a canvas brought to life — like a tourist trap video Van Gogh immersive experience. If the tools at our disposal are grotesque, we had better find a way to make them into art. The thing that makes Jobs finally take his daughter seriously is when she uses his computer to make a painting. What Jobs never reconciles is, what happens when everyone is a painter?

Scott is indeed a useful counterpoint to Boyle. He accepted the knighthood Boyle rejected, bought interest in a film studio rather than create his own school, and has used colonization as a narrative tool rather than a complexity. He tortures and kills his explorer heroes (in the *Alien* movies, *1492*, *Black Hawk Down*), shows the fatal hubris of crusades into 'the unknown' (*Kingdom of Heaven*), and brings down governments and economic systems (*American Gangster, Gladiator, Gladiator II*), but he lacks Boyle's interest in the seductive power of, well, power. The catharsis of having 'made it' like the young lovers of *Slumdog Millionaire*. Boyle's belief in a romantic view of the world means that everyone from the working poor to the hopelessly drug addicted have a shot at redemption ("Choose life," as Renton sarcastically says), whereas Scott has little trouble leaving his characters in the smoking rubble of their own dreams. Just look at their competing versions of the story of the Getty family kidnapping scandal. Scott's movie *All The Money in the World* ends on a note of relief but ambiguity, with the monstrous J. Paul Getty dead, surrounded by his precious works of art, the family narrowly escaping the fate assigned the wealthy. In *Trust,* of which Boyle directed the first three episodes, there are grace notes waiting for everyone, happy endings for nearly every character. Neither sees the best in the world, but one has decided that even the worst of us can — and maybe do — deserve a happy ending.

Steve Jobs is about the man who revolutionized and popularized a different kind of technology, and like Boyle, changed the way we consume information and images. The three parts of the film, set in 1984, 1988, and 1998, are shot on three different film formats (16mm, 35mm, and digital) to separate the realities of each phase of Jobs' professional life. Küchler, who first joined Boyle for *Sunshine* in 2007, worked on film for his first 15 years (his first project was his wife Ngozi Onwurah's afrofuturist *Welcome II The Terrordome*), only beginning to work on hybrid film and digital production with Joe Wright's *Hanna* in 2011. The particular graininess of the 16mm image is alien to Boyle's cinema, which for so long lived in the lowlight of Dod Mantle's early digital darkness and the brilliant colors of Darius Khondji and Brian Tufano's vibrance in his early work. When we're introduced to Steve Jobs in Act I, it's through mirrors and projections. He's trying to make a Macintosh computer speak for itself at a presentation as he refuses to speak to his daughter Lisa, who comes into his life at the same time as his fame as a tech mogul. There is a *TIME* magazine cover that reminds him of his failings. His reflection is notably absent: there is no picture of him, but rather an Eliot-esque 'Empty Man' sitting before a computer, a man without a soul as Jobs threatens to become with every slight he launches at his family and confidantes. Boxes full of copies of the magazine wait for him in an elevator, stacked as tall as he is;

the negative image of Jobs. The man he isn't, the man he won't ever be. But who is he? What is he? Boyle is asking the same thing of himself, but does he know it? Does it matter that the magazine cover was never meant to reflect Jobs, as he learns in the third act? Is there a place for each of us in the culture now?

If Greenaway's biopics reveal his vicious intellect and appreciation for everything *but* the cinema, which was nevertheless his tool, then Boyle's biopics try to reconcile a culture's endless reproduction. In *Pistol* he focuses not on the inspiration that gave us the music and lyrics of Sex Pistols, but the way their relative naïveté allowed them to be commodified. The most important band of the '70s, the band that, by metaphorically consuming the image of Boyle's Olympic leading lady, the Queen of England, changed Britain forever — the way digital cinema would too, two decades later — are in constant struggle with their own vices and their manager's unyielding savvy. The same is true in *Trust,* in which the facts of the Getty family's personal lives compete for narrative space with the deranging effects of their money. Boyle's work is always about money, but after he became the kind of man with largesse enough to give vast sums to charity and to start a film school, he started to wonder what it might do to his outlook by way of his characters. In *Pistol* and *Yesterday,* conflicting visions of popular music, money is like an iron lung, saving lives in exchange for range of movement and a normal life. His body of work is like a refutation of Thomas Carlyle's Great Man Theory — a favorite of screenwriter Sorkin's — in which it is only ragingly imperfect men who change history, whether that's a man stealing Beatles songs or an alienating, autistic control freak like Steve Jobs, who cuts off his daughter and strategically betrays his friends. By turning record company chicanery and inside baseball tech firings into the stuff of high drama, Boyle flattens the thorniness of history as if patting down the hackles of a startled animal. "I'm tired of being treated like Ringo when I know I was John," pleads Steve Wozniak. The names stand out, not just because of what their bearers created, but in spite of how they did it. John Lennon, Steve Jobs, Malcolm McLaren, John Paul Getty — even Aron Ralston, whose only defining traits were his resilience and tolerance for pain — they made history, uncomfortably. Boyle was there to ask what the world looked like in their wake and through their eyes. Like Greenaway, he could engineer a point of view close to how we perceive and remember things, with oblong angles across from the most important moments of our lives, seeing ourselves but not seeing ourselves. "I have been a witness and I tell you, I've been complicit," says Joanna Hoffman. Boyle and *Steve Jobs* specifically ask: what's the difference?

Steve Jobs was born of the culture, in response to it, in defiance of it, to change things through destruction rather than invention. Boyle's creations must split the difference, decoupaging new images with archival footage, commercials, and needle drops. In this way he mirrors Jobs' own cobbling together of a personality and a career identification from the work of other iconoclasts. As Wozniak tells him and Jobs does his best not to hear: "I'm the only one that knows that this guy here is someone you invented." The troubling difference is that Jobs' talent was in orchestrating a vibe and pushing people around. "What do you do?" asks Wozniak, speaking for the audience. More to the point is Lisa's third act insult, "you can talk about the Bauhaus movement and Braun and 'simplicity is sophistication' and Issey Miyake uniforms and Bob Dylan lyrics all you want…" but you're still not a genius. If Boyle and Jobs have something in common, it is a similar wearing of the pins and buttons and t-shirts of geniuses — *Trainspotting*'s worship of Manchester techno and Iggy Pop, *Slumdog Millionaire*'s paeans to Amitabh Bachchan, *Trance*'s Francisco Goya studies. The Beatles and The Sex Pistols each got their own project and Boyle produced *Creation Stories* about the famous indie label Creation Records in 2021. Jobs pulled Dylan and Lennon into his own mythmaking by force (he named his company after the Beatles record label and paid handsomely to 'win' the ensuing legal battles), and Boyle in turn takes Jobs' cultural canonization for his own, as, after all, they both challenged paradigms. *Steve Jobs*' recurring cast of corporate allies and enemies (Wozniak, Hoffman, John Sculley, Andy Hertzfeld) reflects Boyle's own relationships with his collaborators. His falling out with *Trainspotting* star Ewan McGregor, his messy public break-up with *Trance* star Rosario Dawson, his collaboration with boomer Lorax Richard Curtis, his unleashing Alex Garland on the public; the baggage stays the same and the art continues, proof that there is no relationship that can't be sacrificed to genius.

Of course, despite all this, the ending, which never fails to raise the hair on the back of my neck, is a tragedy scored like a triumph. Jobs promises his daughter the iPod, and what that led to wasn't democracy but ownership, not communism but capitalism. One wonders what Lennon, the special guest of the third act of *Yesterday,* would have made of that. Now every phone has Spotify or some other streamer app on it, with access to all the music on Earth for the low cost of endless advertisements, your favorite musicians making pennies per hours streamed, and record companies with more power than they've had since the days of Lennon and Dylan. Almost no one now can rise from nightclub act to epochal artist the way Lennon did on the strength of hard work and talent. Each new update to Jobs' technology took away disc drives, charger cables, headphones, printers, until it was finally the perfect object he wanted to create back in his Silicon Valley garage: a box that's too expensive to buy, too essential not to, that promises everything and does nothing. Boyle's messy cinema of pop culture detritus and addiction meets its ideal in a man who couldn't stop re-making the world. Boyle has the same compulsion. He and David Fincher competed for Best Picture twice, and then he made both a boardroom thriller with a script by Aaron Sorkin like Fincher's *The Social Network,* and a wonky time travel romance like Fincher's *The Curious Case of Benjamin Button.* He made sequels to *Trainspotting* and *28 Days Later...* as if to cement his legacy before anyone else could. He made *Trance,* in which a love of modern art becomes the undoing of a man with a gambling addiction. Boyle can't stop putting it all on red and you risk a lot by making a biopic of someone who may have helped end the world with the technology he made possible to do it. Does he know it? I think he might.

Camera

by Devan Scott

However populist his dramatic sensibilities might lean, Danny Boyle's tack as a formalist is that of a forward-thinking pioneer, willing to employ radical process-based techniques in unusually diverse manners. He does this for two central reasons: first, as an ongoing attempt to escape the restrictions and ossification of conventional studio filmmaking techniques, disrupting the rhythms of film sets as they're commonly practiced. Second, as a fascination with the textural characteristics of any given filmic or digital medium — and in particular with the delta, or formal gap, between those textures, juxtaposed within a single work. These impulses mean that Boyle has been particularly well-situated to take advantage of the new pathways that digital cinema has opened up within the 21st century, in which the toolkits that enable him to follow these impulses have both diversified and miniaturized.

Identifying inflection points in Boyle's career is a difficult task: as an artist famous for hopping between genres, tones, and formal schemes, one could label virtually any of his films as an inflection point of one kind or another. *Steve Jobs*, then, is as good an example as any due to its status as Boyle's final film to be shot (in any significant way) on celluloid film stock. It stands as something of an apex of his play with usage of textural deltas for expressive ends, a tendency that dates back to *Trainspotting*, but whose current manifestation is best understood by starting with his major break from conventional studio working methods at the turn of the century.

Working with his first relatively large budget, a studio looming over his shoulder, a production apparatus that he found both restrictive and unwieldy, and in a remote location, Danny Boyle had by all accounts an absolutely miserable time making *The Beach* in 1999. He later spoke of it in the documentary *Side by Side* as a process that was "too much away from me": the typical means of film production prescribed by the studio system as a sort of terminal, perfected stage of the filmmaking process were, it turns out, largely counter to Boyle's instincts as a filmmaker. A maverick filmmaker choosing to deliber-ately scale down after a fiasco of a large production is a tale as old as the studio system, but such initiatives tend to limit themselves to the world of mise-en-scène and dramatics: fewer locations, performers, and special effects. Boyle, however, was not content to simply scale down within the framework imposed upon him; instead, he set about constructing a new one.

Boyle had seen Tomas Vinterberg's 1998 film *Festen* — the first Dogme 95 film, and arguably the most visually inventive — and found himself so taken with Anthony Dod Mantle's MiniDV-taped-to-a-boom-pole camera operation style that he reached out to him and launched one of digital cinema's great collaborations. After a couple of made-for-TV dry runs, they settled upon *28 Days Later...* as their first major project. Despite their healthy $8 million budget, they elected to shoot the film almost entirely on a set of Canon XL1s, consumer camcorders that recorded in standard-definition resolutions, unfathomably low-fi by celluloid standards.

There was, of course, a very specific practical reason for doing so: the flexibility of having numerous digital cameras placed around a location was the only feasible way in which to record footage of Cillian Murphy wandering around a deserted London without spending catastrophic amounts of money on shutting down traffic in the city center for more than a few minutes at a time. With these cameras, Boyle and Dod Mantle could shoot surreptitiously — illegally — and most importantly subvert the traditional flow of a film set. Boyle was free to design shots with a hitherto unimaginable lack of friction: no more was there a need for a three-person team — at minimum — to set up a bulky 35mm camera on an equally bulky tripod in order to get a frame up.

One might be tempted to think of the extraordinarily low-fidelity aesthetics imposed by these cameras as a necessary evil, but to Boyle and Dod Mantle these divergences from aesthetic convention are not drawbacks to be minimized; they're opportunities to exploit. The infected, in particular, are inseparable from the digital filming and editing techniques used to depict them. The artifice of the edits — jump cuts, speed ramps, freeze frames — and of digital image capture — noise, narrow shutter angles, lens artifacting, infinite depth of field, resolutions so low as to obscure legibility, and bizarre camera placement — define their screen presence as much as anything in the diegesis itself.

The next decade-or-so of Danny Boyle's career saw him expand and iterate upon this process-based philosophy. Despite shooting entirely on celluloid film, Boyle and future *Steve Jobs* cinematographer Alwin H. Küchler took notable steps with the making of *Sunshine* toward the play with formal and textural deltas that would characterize Boyle's most vital subsequent works.

Boyle is not a subtle artist, and as a film in which the sun is a central ongoing visual element, *Sunshine*, perhaps unsurprisingly, makes lens flares a key concern. Küchler and Boyle opted to mix anamorphic and Super 35mm formats — both of which result in mutually distinct flares — as a way of expanding their options for scene-by-scene flare deployment. One scene might feature, as in the case of an early dialogue scene between Murphy and Rose Byrne, prismatic spherical flares that suggest a sort of groggy altered state, while another scene might feature an anamorphic streak to impart additional visual tension to a sun flare.

Boyle's and Küchler's most intense visual gestures revolve around the film's eventual villain, Pinbacker. Like the infected in *28 Days Later…*, he is defined less by his writing and design than he is by the visual and aural elements that accompany him. His Freddie Kreuger–adjacent makeup barely registers, as Küchler and Boyle elect to use an impressive variety of tricks (including a beam-splitting prism to simultaneously record a distorted and non-distorted image via two cameras) to render him as a figure in possession of a sort of gravitational aura, distorting visuals, sounds, and time around him. As far as the film's form is concerned, staring at Pinbacker is akin to staring at the sun.

Slumdog Millionaire represented a dramatic leap into the kaleidoscopic world of mixed digital and celluloid formats for both Boyle and Dod Mantle. By using the Silicon Imaging SI-2K Mini camera system, which featured a sensor block that could be detached from the main body of the camera, Dod Mantle, "separated the camera from his body weight," as Boyle told ASC publication *American Cinematographer*. In practical terms, this extremely lightweight-yet-robust camera system meant that Boyle was about to fulfill each of the requirements he laid out in an October 2007 letter to Dod Mantle:

1.   Following the kids wherever they go
2.   Potential for some secrecy (being at their height)
3.   Letting them carry it sometimes

    4.   Feeling their delicacy and robustness at the
           same time

This system meant a new relationship between the labor of the camera operator and the visible image onscreen was possible — whereas 'handheld' cameras had traditionally been directly attached to the central weight of an operator's body via a shoulder rig or similar, Dod Mantle was able to hold this high-resolution sensor in his hand with virtually no mediating mechanism, aside from a very small gimbal for basic stability.[1] Together, Boyle and Dod Mantle achieved a nearly unprecedented amount of flexibility in movement for a high-resolution imaging system: Dod Mantle's camera was able to peek around corners, zip up and down, and fit into extremely small spaces, all of which are on display during the film's various chases through the streets of Mumbai.

Both *Slumdog Millionaire* and Boyle's follow-up *127 Hours* feature a mix of digital and celluloid imagery that weighs more toward the digital side. Though — if one goes out of one's way to look for these things — there is a visual distinction between the 35mm images and SI-2K images in both of these films. The 2K digital intermediate through which the 35mm film footage was transferred, along with strident color grades applied to all sources, serve to significantly mask these visual differences by rendering the 35mm images in a way that

---

[1] Boyle, for all his punk-rock attitude to camera labor, is keenly aware of micro-vibrations that accompany unstabilized small cameras. In an interview with *The Film Stage*, Dod Mantle described it as "quite unmaverick of him!"

reads as distinctly 'digital' in their textures, thereby blurring the lines between the two.[2]

In both cases — but in *127 Hours* in particular — Boyle's major, medium-based deltas emerge from the distinction between high- and low-fidelity digital. 35mm cameras were deployed not primarily for their aesthetic properties, but because of their superior resolving capabilities in capturing landscapes and plate shots. Similarly, SI-2K cameras were used primarily due to the incredibly space-restricted location in which the bulk of the film takes place, rendering 35mm cameras infeasible. Though Boyle, Dod Mantle, and Enrique Chediak (joining Dod Mantle in DP duties) exploited the intimacy of these cameras to the fullest, Boyle once again saw these mediums not as abstracted aesthetic signifiers but as tools first and foremost: the camera that will *get the shot* is better than the camera that will get the shot with the maximum degree of fidelity possible.

On the other hand: the real Aron Ralston, basis for *127 Hours'* story, had a camera, and it was very much a consumer camcorder. This was all the excuse Boyle needed to frequently mix fidelities, a tendency that only grows more pronounced as Ralston, portrayed by James Franco, descends into desperation, dehydration, and delirium. In post-production, Boyle guided the textural and chromatic elements of the adjustments made to the images based on a scale of "wetness," he told *American Cinematographer* — the early film was wet, saturated,

---

[2] In an era when format emulation mostly runs in one direction, it's all the more startling to see someone essentially emulate a digital image via film stock.

sharp, full of life; late in the movie, the image is soft, desaturated, and often distinctly degraded.

For Boyle, this foregrounding of mixed formats was appropriate for a world of audiences with cameras in their phones. He told *American Cinematographer*: "rather than being locked into the liquid beauty and smoothness of celluloid, people are prepared to see an image fractured by mixed formats." This distinctly contemporary mixing of new and old formats would shortly prove itself most applicable to the story of a man who could claim no small degree of responsibility for the proliferation of these new technologies.

Steve Jobs features a visual structure whose simplicity — three time periods, three shooting formats: 16mm for 1984, 35mm for 1988, Arri Alexa for 1998 — belies all the complexities that such a gesture necessitates. The textural arc of the film tracks the development of Steve Jobs, Apple Computers, and turn-of-the-century culture, and the aesthetic and thematic impact of these formats go well beyond that of mere grain levels.

The 1984 material was shot with Kodak Vision3 500T 7219 film stock. "One of the wonderful side effects of the 16mm," Küchler told *American Cinematographer*, "is that it looks aesthetically raw and poetically beautiful, which mirrors the story of Steve Jobs [in his early years] perfectly where the original ideas are there but not fully formed." The look is one not only associated with the out-of-control — the chaos of the grain (an expression of randomness in silver halide form) an externalization of the onscreen events — but of the handmade: decades of prior films have trained audiences to associate the perceptual qualities of 16mm film stocks with a certain mode of production at certain budgets, and so a sense of struggle and the aura of the low-budget is embedded in the texture of the image.

Boyle saw the progression of one epoch — and format — to the next as a series of incremental upgrades in "visual quality"; the markedly sharper 35mm Kodak 5219 film stock used for the 1988 scenes sees Jobs midway through developing the visual language that would be his popular legacy. Here Boyle's visual textures may be more 'refined,' but they're still deliberately bound by the celluloid-based faktura of the past: the physicality of the film stock itself. In parallel, Jobs in this second act has not yet made his great 'leap' into his own unique, plastic, and antiseptic design philosophy: he, too, is still bound by the technology and forms of the 'old.'

The last act of *Steve Jobs* sees Boyle texturally embodying the design philosophy that would come to define Apple in the last years of Jobs' life: the jump from 35mm to Arri Alexa is one into what Boyle called "a world of precision and infinite possibility." The image is conspicuously grainless, as if a layer of mediation has been wiped away. What's left is not an absence of texture but a presence of an actively clean and sterile one: the world of Apple circa 1998 is now one of total, end-to-end control, all elements smoothed out except for the ones that Mr. Jobs has personally curated. His antiseptic and minimalist design language not only governs his company and branding — and therefore the mise-en-scène — but also the texture of the film itself: one nearly gets the sense that he is personally curating every last element of the images we're now seeing.

In an indication as to the complex knock-on effects of this sort of play with mediums, Steadicam operator Geoffrey Haley found that the physical weight of each shooting format impacted his operation in ways that were luckily appropriate for each of the eras depicted. "Traditionally, the heavier the rig, the more stable the Steadicam behaves," he told ASC's publication. "The 16mm camera was nice and light and I was able to do longer takes, but [it was] also a little more skittish." However intentional or otherwise, this evolutionary path tracks the arc of Jobs as a character — and *Steve Jobs* as a wider textural work — perfectly. Jobs' immaturity in Act I is mirrored in the relatively rough and weightless camera operation enforced by a light rig on a Steadicam; the Arri Alexa's palpable smoothness caused by its total lack of moving parts, likewise, mirrors Jobs' total control during Act III, with the heavy 35mm camera providing something of a middle ground during Act II.

Of course, *Steve Jobs* — the movie as well as the man — is but a microcosm: this format-based arc draws parallels to the nature of technological evolution and modernity. Celluloid is old. Celluloid is the Apple II. We've moved past that: we're in iPhone land now, the land of dematerialized media. Film stock, like vinyl records, is the physical; the new ways are quantized, data-based. And yet the film is not blind to these trade-offs: for every layer of perceptual mediation stripped away, so too is a certain degree of what we might perceive as the 'organic' or the handmade. Control and minimalism might carry with them a sort of dehumanization and detachment from material reality. *Steve Jobs* as a film seems ambivalent about these trade-offs, but it is a telling indicator that Boyle has not shot on film since; he has instead elected to explore the limits of digital imaging workflows.

⁎⁎⁎

In 2025, *28 Years Later* came at a point when the supposed trade-off that Boyle and Dod Mantle made in the course of making *28 Days Later...* — image 'quality' for freedom — is now largely moot. Boyle could have elected to shoot *28 Years Later* on a series of (to pick one of many options) FX3 mirrorless cameras, which feature all of the freedom associated with early MiniDV cameras, but with data harvesting capabilities far more in-line with 35mm film stock and modern, high-end digital cameras.

And yet his impulses led him elsewhere: Boyle told Dod Mantle that *28 Days Later...* was a particularly satisfying moment of unity between form and content, and expressed a desire to somehow get back there — but recontextualized for our current era. This led them to iPhones, and moreover iPhones with a series of modifications and attachments that serve to degrade and distort the resultant images. Dod Mantle expressed the creative process as such in an interview with Nick Newman for *The Film Stage*:

> "[F]or Danny, it was a basic idea that this small tool — something that could be lying in the field 28 years later in Britain — could render images. It's not, you know, a philosophical point, but that a thing like that — just a remnant of the society — could be used to make a $75 million studio film, so it would help it in its sheen to feel and look and behave differently, and he knows me well enough to know that that will induce me to do things differently because I inevitably have to."

That inducement is at the heart of what makes Boyle's cinema so formally exciting: he and his collaborators are unusually willing to choose unconventional toolkits and *listen* to them — technology informing art and vice versa — to understand what they can do, can't do, and how they change the dynamics of producing films.

Performance

by Sarah Jae Leiber

I have a Computer Dad who was always Doing Something On The Computer while I was growing up. I'd stand behind him as he fiddled with Photoshop, creating branding for his fantasy baseball team, or downloaded the latest power pop albums from shady websites that always looked like bigger-deal hacker domains to my eyes, or read inappropriate-for-me movie reviews on *Ain't It Cool News*, certain that someday I would grow up and be Doing Something On The Computer while my own child looked on. In my fantasy, I would never be Doing Something on my own — I would share whatever was going on with that child, and teach them to navigate the expansive internet as a fellow traveler. I became Very Online Very Young as a means of continuing the family business.

Steve Jobs had a daughter named Lisa, played by three actresses (Makenzie Moss, Ripley Sobo, and Perla Haney-Jardine) at three ages over the course of Danny Boyle's and Aaron Sorkin's *Steve Jobs*. Lisa had a

Computer Dad who was always Doing Something On The Computer, though it seems to me that she never really got to be in the inner sanctum of her dad's Computer Doing. She never got to stand over his shoulder and wonder what was going on. She barely got to stand in the same room as him.

I went to acting school, probably as a byproduct of growing up in a house where I had to fight the computer or the TV for my parents' attention. Part of my early acting training was status exercises. We learned that performers can play high or low status to affect the dynamic of the scene, depending on how their character would approach interaction with the people around them. A high-status player like a king or queen might "raise self to lower partner," forcing their scene partner into a lower-status mode by nature of their raw power. A low-status player like a royal servant might "raise partner to lower self" in the event that the king or queen they serve needs to be coddled into the status quo.[1] Status is basically a performance of self-esteem, wielded for good and evil.

As Jobs, Michael Fassbender is always playing high status, and he is, most of the time, raising self to lower scene partner. Like a king. Mere mortals are the ones who oscillate between presumed authority and supplication, changing the way they interact with people to suit what they need to get out of conversations. As

---

[1] A college friend once described me as "the lowest-status player of all time," constantly moving around with my head hanging down to ensure no one would ever get mad at me or treat me badly.

genius creator-god, Jobs never stoops, never spooks, and never allows his colleagues, friends, or family to believe he even has a low status mode.

That's what makes Jobs' interactions with Lisa so juicy and so distinct from his other relationships in the film. We see Jobs berate others into submission, belittling coworkers and co-creators and other adults whose status could theoretically match or mirror his. But Jobs doesn't stop raising self to lower scene partner when the scene partner is a child — his child. It gives away the game. When Jobs lowers Lisa to raise himself, he looks pathetic, not powerful. Steve Jobs is not a genius creator-god; for most of the movie, he can't even admit to having created his own daughter, because looking an imperfect human invention in the face is significantly harder than putting her name on a product.

Fassbender's Jobs doesn't have time for anyone who is not operating exactly on his level. Sorkin's famous walk-and-talks slot right into the propulsive force of Jobs' will; we spend most of this movie in hallways and green rooms in the moments before giant product launches, watching Jobs' lackeys make the impossible possible. Jobs is particularly curt, abrasive, and self-mythmaking in interactions with people like Andy Hertzfeld (Michael Stuhlbarg) and Steve Wozniak (Seth Rogen), people he sees as grunts, not creative visionaries; with other computer people, perhaps to mask his lack of practical knowledge, it is especially important for Fass-bender-as-Jobs to raise self by lowering scene partner.

Kate Winslet is a particularly adept status chameleon in this movie, playing Joanna Hoffman as someone who can quickly adapt to changing circumstances. As a marketing executive, Hoffman's eye for detail and narrative is supplemented by her skill as a people person and manager of personalities. She is Jobs' work wife, with all the tired eyes and hurried apologies for his behavior that entails. She'll even iron his shirts for him. Winslet dovetails between playing professional and playing nurturer, changing tactics on a dime if the last one has stopped working.

Winslet-as-Hoffman wields her high status as a much more pliable tool than Fassbender-as-Jobs ever does; Hoffman knows how to use status to make other people feel good, and she sees actual utility in that. Early on, when Jobs is manipulating his employees toward committing some degree of fraud while in the same breath denying paternity of his five-year-old daughter to her face, Hoffman gets down on Lisa's level and asks her if she'll help her make the computer say hello. This lowering of self to raise scene partner's status is incredibly humanizing. In contrast to what Fassbender is doing this early on in Act I of the film, it is practically parenting.

It is easy for children to play low status against adults; they are inherently powerless against elders, politically and socially and performance-wise. Lisa's sweet, quiet, observational nature at this point in her life makes it particularly heartbreaking to watch Jobs refuse to lower himself to meet her at her level as he walks around like he's made of brain and no heart. Late in this first interaction, though, Jobs has Lisa demonstrate her value, putting his hand over hers to show her how to wield the controls. He is using her, of course; Lisa is a means to an end here, a way to prove to the public that using his computer is so easy a bastard can do it. But Lisa discovers MacPaint and disarms him, using his product fluently to create something meaningful on her first try.

In this moment, Lisa is raising herself to lower her scene partner in a way that's about equivalence more than it is about control; Jobs is not yet interested in raising Lisa up, but this does level him to the point where he agrees to start paying Lisa and her mother a livable wage in child support. Status play is about how we influence and impact the people around us — Lisa, let into her Computer Dad's inner sanctum for the first time, finds part of her power in his acknowledgement. When she asks him, "Can you teach me more things? On the computer?" we can tell this is the closest she's come to being embraced by her father.

Part of status play is the acknowledgement that sometimes your raising and lowering tactics do not work on the scene partner. You can attempt to lower somebody by raising yourself, but their self-esteem and power in the character plays a factor in how your try is received. There are not many people who can successfully lower Fassbender's Jobs; a notable exception is Jeff Daniels as John Sculley, who holds the power of the purse that allows Jobs to take the kind of risks he needs to innovate. In Daniels-as-Sculley's hands, we can see desperation in Fassbender-Jobs; we can also see the desire to please and the terror in disappointment.

Steve Jobs is about chaotic family units — Jobs runs Apple like a fucked-up family, with toxic dynamics that trick people into staying. Daniels-as-Sculley plays the role of Jobs' father, who both giveth and taketh away his blessing and his support. When Jobs feels betrayed by Sculley, he becomes single-mindedly interested in making Sculley feel just as small. Status is a push and pull, even in the most extreme of cases.

Sculley's stern, tough love contrasts with Jobs' relationship with Lisa, which is both stern and tough, but contains no love that lowers the self for the majority of the film. In Act II, when Lisa is a bright and inquisitive fourth grader (Sobo) trying desperately to keep up with her dad (Sorkin's pitter-patter dialogue is an asset here), Jobs asks her why she keeps asking him the same questions, unaware that those questions are Lisa lowering herself to raise up her father. She asks questions because she wants her father to explain the answers to her, and she wants her father to explain the answers to her because she wants him to care about the things she knows. She wants her Computer Dad to teach her how to be interesting enough to be paid attention to.

Steve Jobs was a victim of the broken American adoption system, given up at birth and bounced around between two families before he was adopted by people his birth mother did not initially approve of. In acting-speak, this is the given circumstance of Jobs' life that contextualizes all of his extreme behavior — at least, that is how Sorkin writes it. Jobs' drive comes from his feelings of physical and emotional abandonment, and his high status masks an inherent mistrust that he will be taken care of regardless of how well he performs. Jobs raises self to lower scene partner as a survival tactic, needing to be good enough to annihilate a subconscious fear of being left alone.

It takes colossal failure to humble Jobs, and it takes rebuilding himself to meet his daughter at her level. By the time Lisa is in college in Act III (and played by Haney-Jardine), she has given up trying to be nice and compliant to catch her dad's ear. She has learned to raise self by lowering partner, refusing to let Jobs look away from the chaos he has caused in her and her mother's lives. "I'm not impressed with your story, Dad," Lisa says. "It's that you knew and you didn't do anything about it and that makes you an unconscionable coward." Jobs withholds Lisa's college tuition when she allows her mother to sell the house he bought them, and is generally cruel when things do not shake out his way or make him look like a demigod with an unfortunate daughter. We learn alongside Jobs that Lisa has had a wide cadre of people at her disposal who have been consistently interested in her success. Jobs' coworkers, who are the closest thing he has to a real family, have taken care of Lisa's emotions and her physical needs in lieu of her father's attention; Hoffman has especially stepped in to help Lisa handle her emotions, and Hertzfeld is even paying her college tuition.

Instead of destroying him, for the first and only time

in his relationship with Lisa, this revelation – coupled with Lisa's verbal acuity, wielded to hurt him deeply and specifically – simply lowers Jobs' status. He follows her up to the roof and confirms to her that the Lisa computer was named after her. He sees the Walkman on her hip and tells her he wants to put a thousand songs in her pocket. He tells her he doesn't know why he has been a bad father to her, other than the fact that he's "poorly made." And he shows her the printout of that first piece of art Lisa made on MacPaint back when she was five, that he's kept with him all of these years. At the end of *Steve Jobs*, Fassbender tips his hand into humanity by lowering himself to raise his scene partner — the kind of subversion that recontextualizes and makes richer everything we have already seen. Lowering himself allows him to see his daughter for the first time. In response, Lisa changes her tactic, too.

Music

by Charlie Brigden

Steve Jobs is an opera driven by music scored, needle-dropped, and discussed. In a *Huffington Post* interview, composer Daniel Pemberton said of the biopic's subject that "There is not one side of music that could reflect his personality. There is a classical side to him, a rebellious side to him, a technical side to him, a soft side to him, and a cold side to him." Jobs' internal and external idiosyncrasies reflected a complicated and not-always-in-time rhythm, best expressed without words.

Director Danny Boyle and writer Aaron Sorkin split the narrative into three sections, which Boyle called "Vision," "Revenge," and "Wisdom." Each section had its own time period and its own aesthetic, which meant music could be used as an efficient way to set the tone of the act and accompany the transitions from year to year. The composer of the score would be responsible for the music during the act, while songs would be an ideal way of transitioning between the acts and the time periods.

Boyle's films were already known for featuring

existing music front and center, most famously in *Trainspotting* with Iggy Pop's "Lust for Life." Sorkin's *Steve Jobs* script called for the use of specific tracks in transitional moments and built a moment of bonding out of Joni Mitchell's "Both Sides, Now" — a song referenced in Walter Isaacson's biography as something Jobs would contemplate. Isaacson's *Steve Jobs*, the movie's official source material, also tells of Jobs' obsession with Bob Dylan, from the early days when he and Steve Wozniak would hunt down bootlegs of Dylan concerts in Northern California to his quoting of lyrics in his speeches. The man who reshaped how we all experience music was shaped in turn by the music of his time.

Pemberton already had an extensive career in television, but by 2015 had worked on few feature films. Among those few were Ridley Scott's *The Counselor*, which drew Boyle to Pemberton's style, per *Deadline*. Pemberton also had a love of vintage music hardware, which would be essential to capturing some of the period style music required in the first act.

For Act I, they decided to write music using synthesizers, with a catch: the hardware would only be synths that were available around the time of the first act's keynote speech. "We kind of had this idea that the first act, set in 1984, should embrace this optimism of the future... and the potential of computing," Pemberton told MPA's *The Credits*. "I wanted to use the synthesizer because I felt that was an instrument worthy of the era, and again, it was this very new exciting sound.

It promised the future, but now actually sounds almost retro." The composer was forced to work differently for the first act: "Those kinds of limitations can be very effective," he said in an interview published by the Tribeca Film Festival.

Act I also introduces Jobs' love of Dylan backstage with then-CEO of Apple John Sculley. Jobs evaluates which lyrics from Dylan's iconic 1964 cut of "The Times They Are A-Changin'" to quote in his keynote. The song is a defined part of the movie's DNA — in the finished film, the lyrics suddenly appear projected on the backstage environment. Sorkin, in his screenplay, even envisioned the song as the first transitional song between acts:

```
'The Times They Are a-Changin'' crashes
in.

But this isn't Bob Dylan's version--it's
a woman singing and instead of an
acoustic guitar it's a slightly fuller
and slightly more up-tempo arrangement.
It's not a Vietnam-era protest song but a
more contemporary and literal statement.
```

It's possible the version Sorkin mentions in the script is the 1967 recording by Cher, but either way, Boyle thought it was too obvious, he told *Newsweek*, especially after Jobs' discussion of the lyrics earlier in the scene. The final film uses "Rainy Day Women #12 and 35" from Dylan's *Blonde On Blonde*, which nicely subverts expectations. "We changed it to 'Rainy Day Women' and it suited it perfectly," Boyle said. "Nothing is as good as that, really... It's slightly disarming as well. What is coming is an act; [Jobs] is actually full of cunning. He's got a very hidden agenda... I thought it just puts you off-guard."

As the film moves into 1988, it takes on a dramatic and truly operatic nature, both thematically and aesthetically. Here, Pemberton uses a full orchestra for Act II and the launch of the NeXT Computer. "It's all set inside the San Francisco Opera House," Pemberton told Tribeca, "so it was a great way to reflect those surroundings and explore the idea of Steve Jobs as the conductor of the orchestra as well as the ringmaster of this insane circus. That felt like a very flamboyant and dramatic way to tell the story."

The dramatic, and subsequently musical, focus is on two conversations: Jobs and Sculley and Jobs and his daughter Lisa, now nine years old. Pemberton described hearing Boyle talk about the second act centered on an act of revenge, "like a Shakespearean tragedy." The track underscoring Jobs' argument with Sculley — titled "Revenge" — "was probably the biggest challenge of the entire film," according to Pemberton. The score and the words weave together intricately as Jobs and Sculley fight in the present and past, the film relentlessly inter-cutting. "It was incredibly difficult," Pemberton told cultural magazine *PopMatters*. "You're basically writing a 10-minute symphony that has to have complete musicality, rather than just score, but at the same time, it has to respond to everything that's happening in the picture, which was constantly being tweaked and re-edited." Describing the sequence's development, Sorkin said in an audio commentary, "At the outset, this was a section... that we had a little bit of a problem with, and then something happened where it turned into one of the best parts of the movie." "You have to not impose yourself too heavily," Pemberton commented to *PopMatters*, "and sometimes, actually, writing the more minimal music that's very subtle is very difficult, because it needs to have identity. It needs to have a kind of sense of emotional storytelling. It needs to have a lot of space."

The other pivotal conversation of Act II takes place on a catwalk with Lisa. It doesn't feature a song (you might catch some notes coming from her headphones in the sound mix of an earlier scene), but it is about the music on Lisa's Walkman: "Both Sides, Now." Joni Mitchell wrote the song in 1966, but it was made famous by Judy Collins, who recorded it the following year. Not fond of Collins' upbeat version, Mitchell recorded it herself for her 1969 album *Clouds*. It's more stripped down and intimate, and has a greater sense of reflection and, as Lisa says, regret.

Jobs finds Lisa seemingly hiding in the Opera House rafters and, amid all the arguments and chaos in the minutes before a sure-to-flop launch, tries to connect with his daughter. He asks Lisa what she's listening to and she tells him, "I'm listening to two versions of the same song. And then when I get to the end I rewind and listen to them again. It's the same song but the versions are different." Sorkin's stage direction notes, "STEVE holds a moment... then sees an opening." And a father lets his daughter tell him about the music she listens to.

The conversation, during which Lisa compares the two versions of "Both Sides, Now" as "girlish" and "regretful," was inspired by a description of her father in Isaacson's book. Per his biographer, Jobs would listen to the song on his iPod, noting that it's "interesting how people age." Interestingly, the track Jobs was listening to then was a later version Joni Mitchell recorded in 2000, with much lusher and fuller orchestrations. Curiously, though, in Sorkin's script, the second version Lisa listens to is revealed to be a different arrangement altogether. We assume the two tracks are Collins' and Mitchell's versions, but the script (which had the song playing over the credits of the movie) describes what is presumably the "regretful" recording as "a beautiful male/female duet with heartbreaking harmonies, more mature, wiser and haunted." This version is from 1991, and a collaboration between Irish band Clannad and British singer Paul Young. Originally recorded for Blake Edwards' gender-swap comedy *Switch*, the song has transcended its origins and become a much-respected version of Mitchell's classic.

Boyle's choice for the transition into 1998 was another deviation from the script. Sorkin's choice was another perhaps too obvious cut: George Frideric Handel's 1741 oratorio *Messiah*, specifically the finale of Scene 3, "For unto us a child is born," based on a verse from Isaiah interpreted by Christians to be about the birth of Jesus, the "Prince of Peace." Sorkin chose an interesting version of Handel's piece in the one recorded by American vocal trio The Roches for their 1990 album of Christmas songs, *We Three Kings*.

Boyle's replacement was a simple one – "Don't Look Back Into the Sun," by British band The Libertines, with its melodic UK indie soundwave, provides an exciting musical backdrop for the return of the prodigal son to Apple. "There's absolutely no justification for that," Boyle told *Newsweek*. "I'd love to be able to tell you there's a Libertines connection to the digital revolution, but sadly I cannot."

Act III, "Wisdom," is a kind of redemption story, with commercial and personal successes for Jobs, but it also has a bittersweet tone because of the decisions he made to get there, and the pieces he has to pick up. Suitably, the score has an unobtrusive feel, becoming ambient at times. With the launch of the iMac and the concept of the iPod floating unnamed in the future, the music was appropriately composed digitally on Apple hardware. "In the third act," Pemberton told *Clash Music*, "it's 1998 and computers have become as powerful as we were promised they would be in 1984. And I write everything on a Mac, I use Apple software and I think one of the things that's amazing about Steve Jobs and Apple is they were the first people of influence in technology, I feel, who really understood the artistic potential of technology and computing."

Pemberton described using the computer as an expressive tool:

> "It allows me to be so much more powerful as an individual
> and as an artist, I wanted to kind of embrace that for the

> third act and start off writing a more digital score, which
> was kind of in the computer and it also reflects Steve's
> personality at this point – it's a very ambient, cold, intro-
> spective, emotive act in the film where he kind of realizes
> that to get to where he gets to at that point he has to make
> various sacrifices and choices."

It is in this act when Jobs finally embraces being a father, in a moment accompanied by a reprise of the "Child" motif from the opening act — played two notes at a time, one fleeting, the other lingering — only in this digital, warmer tone, matching the evolution of Jobs' emotions along with the evolution of the Mac, technology, and sound. In the film's emotional climax, Jobs does what he's been teasing and avoiding for so long: he connects with his daughter through art and through technology — his medium — promising to get rid of Lisa's clunky Walkman and replace it with a magic trick. At this point in Sorkin's script, "Both Sides, Now" would have started, but in the film, Boyle introduces the soft strains of The Maccabees' "Grew Up at Midnight." "That was Danny," said Pemberton to *PopMatters*. "Danny loves that song."

As the film ends, we return to Bob Dylan and his track "Shelter From the Storm," from 1975's *Blood On the Tracks*, again chosen by Danny Boyle. "I kind of sense a loss in 'Shelter From the Storm,'" he said, describing the song to *Newsweek* as "rather beautiful at the end." He continued, "When you leave the theater, it's no longer 1998. You're back in 2015 — and [Lisa's] dad's gone. So there's a kind of loss there. He lost out on her, for a section of her life. It involved that feeling. It's

like not knowing what you have until it's gone, really."
Like Jobs, the sense is elusive and complicated — best
expressed without words.

Edit

by Alexander B. Joy

Neither the format, setting, nor structure of Aaron Sorkin's screenplay for *Steve Jobs* were conducive to the propulsive forward motion that moviegoers expect. The repetitive three-act structure, centered around Jobs' last-minute preparations for three different product launches, lacked the dramatic variety of a less stringently partitioned production. The crowded, constrained settings (consisting of green rooms, backstage passages, auditorium wings, and the like) inhibited adventurous camerawork and other movement-based strategies for enhancing visual interest. And, of course, the action — such as it is — amounted to nothing but talk. Speaking to *Variety*, editor Elliot Graham observed that he had to contend with one key question: "How do you keep the momentum going so you don't outstay your welcome, when there is such repetition?"

Graham's ingenious solution was to approach the editing of the film as though it belonged to a completely different genre than the theatre-inspired biopic. He approached each of the film's three acts based on the intuition that the screenplay felt like an "action film with words," as he told *Film Doctor*, or like "a series of fight sequences" to *Variety*, and opted to treat conversation as combat, with the appropriate sense of kinetic energy. The strategy is apparent in the speed and arrangement of the film's many exchanges, where each shot and reverse-shot, especially during heated moments, lands like a thrust or parry. The end result is that *Steve Jobs*, by virtue of its editing, causes each act to read like a prize fight in which Jobs is competing — and for the overall film to wind up an unusual fusion of biopic and pugilism picture.

Unusual as it may seem, *Steve Jobs* is the spiritual successor of Martin Scorsese's *Raging Bull*, a biopic about the onetime middleweight boxing champion, Jake LaMotta. *Raging Bull* charts the vicissitudes of LaMotta's life and career, from his climb to the middleweight title to his later life as a divorced, obese, financially and legally troubled club emcee. Yet the film adopts an unconventional narrative structure: it treats major boxing matches from LaMotta's fighting career as the key events of his life, making them the fulcrums of the domestic and business dramas that bookend them. The function of each match is to reveal what the material on either side of them means; the character (and character arc) of the fraught, inarticulate LaMotta is made intelligible in the ring. Much as *Steve Jobs* tells the story of its title character through product reveals, *Raging Bull* refracts and clarifies LaMotta through the lens of his fights, imbuing recurring elements (same blood, same sport, same violence, etc.) with evolving meanings by adopting a new editorial approach for each new context. Each fight hits differently, in all senses of the phrase.

The same structure and storytelling principles that inform *Raging Bull* map neatly onto *Steve Jobs*. "One of the things [director Danny Boyle] wanted every department head to do," Graham told *Film Doctor*, "was to find every way possible to differentiate the acts," ostensibly as a way to add texture and variation to the static film Sorkin had written. To distinguish the acts in conjunction with (or despite) the script, the *Steve Jobs* team tapped the rest of the filmmaker's toolkit — in particular, the visual repertoire. For Graham's department, that meant ensuring that each act was edited with a different cadence and logic than the others. "We were trying to create a cinematic language rather than only a linguistic language," said Graham. As a result of these efforts, the three acts of *Steve Jobs* are, as Graham noted to *Variety*, effectively "three stories." As with *Raging Bull*, the editing transforms the film's repeating elements with each new context, providing widely divergent accounts of what each of Jobs' product launches means at and for each phase of his career — if not his life as a whole.

A close reading of the three acts through an editorial lens reveals a separate genre register at work each time. These genre framings complicate — or counter outright — the narrative Jobs attempts to construct in each act.

And all throughout, the skillful editing primes audiences to puncture the mythos that Jobs tries to cultivate around himself. In this light, *Steve Jobs* becomes less an ode to the "visionary" entrepreneur than a study of how reality intrudes on such a person's dreams and delusions alike.

Three figures huddle over a computer, unable to convince the machine to speak. One figure is Steve Jobs, the film's eponymous, polarizing tech figure; he insists that, no matter what, the computer (the soon-to-be-unveiled Apple Macintosh) must use its buzzing digital voice to greet the audience of the forthcoming product launch. The second figure, engineer Andy Hertzfeld, informs Jobs over and over again that his request is impossible to fulfill within such a tight timeframe. And the third, marketing chief Joanna Hoffman, flails desperately for a satisfactory alternative to the voice sample that will placate Jobs. The setup captures in miniature the core question behind *Steve Jobs*: Can a computer be made to say anything on behalf of its creator? In one respect, the answer is 'no.' Jobs' beloved "Hello" sample is not brought off as intended, having to rely instead on a model with more memory than the one being demoed, and the resolution of the first act hinges on the kind of willful misrepresentation for which tech companies (and Jobs himself) are infamous. But in a different regard, the Macintosh's silence does indeed say something about Jobs — blasting him by making plain all he cannot do despite his limitless self-assurance. And the editing of the film brings that critique to the surface, placing Jobs in a genre where hubris such as his seldom goes unpunished.

To this end, Act I incorporates a visual language typically associated with thrillers. It features quick and choreographic camerawork, leaning on rapid cuts that bounce between people at conversational loggerheads, and swinging movements that take in the full scope of a space in one dexterous sweep. These lively maneuvers establish a swift, aggressive pace, such that most sequences in the first act trace an energy thrown about the room like the momentum of a landed punch. Yet no blow is struck, for all combat in *Steve Jobs* is ultimately verbal, the ricochet of information traveling at the speed of thought. It creates a rapid ratcheting of conflict, tension, and revelation consistent with thriller standards, wherein every new insight raises the stakes, and adds new anxieties rather than disarming them.

The thriller framing is important because of the characterization it grants the dramatic questions that power the first act. In a vacuum, the act's main conflicts read like the standard plot contrivances that keep an audience interested in the proceedings. Will Jobs pull off his tech demo? Will the "Hello" voice sample actually work? Will Jobs' questionable product design prove a computational or commercial failure? Will his morally suspect advertising choices and logistically unsound business decisions come back to bite him? Will his grandiose sales promises come true? Many other genre contexts would present these as stories of the hero taking on the world, of the luminary showing the uninitiated something new, and the drama hinging on whether they have the eyes to see as he does. In such narratives, ends justify means; a successful mission forgives the hero's worst choices (like, say, hiring skinheads as extras in television ads). Casting the stories in terms of a thriller, however, removes their heroic aspect, replacing the presumption of success with the knowledge that all of Jobs' showpieces are fundamentally deceptions. The question of whether Jobs will manage to deliver a flawless tech demo is dramatic here not because his victory would usher in a better or more enlightened world, but because we know it's predicated on lies regarding what his new computer can do. (A different machine is ultimately required to deliver the voice sample, after all.) The stakes behind Jobs' wildly optimistic sales projections are less that they could herald a new age of computing, and more that they threaten to expose his delusions regarding the tech ecosystem and the people who constitute it. In effect, the tension inherent in each plot thread comes from wondering when — or whether — Jobs' lies will be exposed. The Silicon Valley myth surrounding the real-life Steve Jobs is that he was a magician, creating inimitable product styles and loyal customer bases where none existed before. But a magician is one who works magic, and the first act's genre framing argues that the protagonist of *Steve Jobs* is no such person. He's an illusionist at best, a weaver of mirages who amounts to yet another species of con man.

In this light, the first act assigns Jobs a curious characterization: He may be the central figure, but he's also the villain. With the dramatic engine of Act I being the question of how long his cons can withstand scrutiny, Jobs is presented like the quarry in a "howdunit"[1] whom everyone is on the verge of exposing. In part, this is evident in his defensive behavior. Jobs' dialogue throughout Act I is most often a series of deflections and denials intended to force those around him to see the world as he dictates. For example, beyond adamantly refusing to acknowledge paternity of his daughter Lisa, he also concocts logically tortured mathematical formulas that supposedly disprove he's her father. It's not enough for him that he alone deny Lisa's parentage — all the world must be made to agree with him, too. Additionally, when his business partner Steve Wozniak makes the modest request that Jobs acknowledge some key engineers of the company's then-flagship Apple II during his pivotal keynote address, Jobs won't consent to it. The financial backing and infrastructural support that those team members helped provide count for nothing before Jobs' studiously cultivated image, since their existence alone undercuts his pretensions of independence and control.

The editing serves to underscore Jobs' disproportionately adversarial reaction to these normal adult pressures.

---

[1] For instance, the television series *Columbo* or *Poker Face*.

He's often shown among backstage or green room settings, such that the temptation would be to depict him like a performer in preparation. Yet the shot composition conveys none of that glamour. Instead, they emphasize the proximity of walls and ceilings, frequently showing Jobs in places of maximum physical constraint. The space matches his headspace; the perspectives of other people enclose and threaten him. As a result, Jobs often looks like a predatory creature stalking a cage — dangerous to approach, and even more dangerous to release. It makes for a clever parallel with *Raging Bull*'s opening sequence, in which LaMotta paces the ring like a zoo animal on display. But it also captures the act's core idea that Jobs is an embattled malefactor. "I'm like Julius Caesar," Jobs complains later on, "I'm surrounded by enemies" — seemingly forgetting or omitting that Caesar was a dictator whose death by stabbing had ample justification.

Like the storied Roman politician, the Jobs of Act I finds himself in a situation where cuts work against him. Inspired editorial choices sabotage Jobs' stated aspirations and undermine the validity of his reasoning. The core design principles behind the Macintosh double as a portrait of Jobs and his desires; he insists upon "a closed system, end-to-end control, completely incompatible with anything," encapsulating both his obsessive, fastidious mindset and the total subordination he covets. Even so, the editing denies him what he's after. Jobs presumes that the "closed system" offers a measure of comfort to a user base that would be intimidated by seeing the components of the computer. However, we're shown that access to the inner workings of a complex system is precisely what instills that missing comfort and confidence. During a particularly public argument outside his dressing room, when the camera pans to reveal Jobs' onlookers rooted in silence and terror, their fear is owed to his mind's impenetrable operations; unable to predict how the volatile Jobs will re/act, they can only cower in expectation of the worst.

Elsewhere, Jobs contends that his unusual computer model will succeed because "[people] don't know what they want until you show them." Yet this premise runs counter to the proceedings of the entire act. Jobs' most intricate (or insane) assertions regarding reality as he perceives it are bookended by cuts to others — namely, Hoffman, Wozniak, and Jobs' spurned girlfriend Chrisann Brennan — who are all articulate in and of their wants, but whom Jobs bulldozes and ignores when their stated desires are contrary to his. The foundational lie of Jobs' con is that he knows people better than they do themselves. But, much as he repackages a modified Unix as a proprietary operating system, he is merely trying to pass narcissism off as insight.

As a result of the editing's steady skepticism toward Jobs, when the big Macintosh launch nears, the mood feels inconclusive. We have not been primed to consider it a deserved, heroic accomplishment. If anything, the prevailing attitude when Jobs prepares to take the stage is a sense of unfairness. We know Jobs is pulling one over on his audience, and since Act I has set him up to be eminently unlikable, the prospect of his victory is bitter to contemplate. It leaves us hungering for him to face some kind of comeuppance — soon to arrive in the form of his ouster from Apple. Cleverly enough, the momentary dissatisfaction that the editing has produced is how the film bridges the emotional and narrative gap between the otherwise self-contained first and second acts. Ensuring that viewers desire consequences for Jobs' unjust actions also guarantees that they remain tuned in to the film despite the structural lull of the first act's conclusion. The momentum carries; the editing overcomes the regimentation of the script.

The pursuit of consequences entices us along for the second act. However, in order to avoid tonal and thematic repetition, *Steve Jobs* shifts its editorial style in Act II. The accompanying change in genre framing not only reconfigures how we receive Jobs, but redefines the arc of the entire film.

The second act revolves around a MacGuffin of sorts: the NeXT Computer, AKA the "Black Cube," Jobs' latest computer model, portrayed as a literal and figurative black box — opaque, impenetrable, inscrutable. What few indicators we receive as to its contents hint that it is poised to be, as Wozniak remarks, "the single biggest failure in the history of personal computing." Viewers are invited to join the film's characters in questioning every aspect of Jobs' bizarre little prism. What's inside? What does it do? What *will* it do? (An outright technical failure remains one potential outcome for this, the least-known of the devices presented in the film.) Meanwhile, similar questions pursue Jobs himself throughout the act. Given that the film's first leg portrayed him as a fastidious, controlling perfectionist, it seems unthinkable that he would march, upright and willing, into the launch of an unfinished product that is doomed to fail. What is his game — or endgame?

Such puzzles drive the middle segment of *Steve Jobs*, and the entire second act is edited accordingly, channeling the cues and conventions of mystery films. The editing toys with the audience's focus, repeatedly feinting and misdirecting around details that purport to offer vital information. Yet the editorial legerdemain still provides all the necessary components for the solution, and — like any good mystery — the rationale behind every move and mechanism coheres come the end of the act.

In a major deviation from the language of Act I, the shots in Act II are often significantly slower. The combative cadence of the shot/reverse-shot pairings from before (except for a crucial sequence later on) is largely set aside in favor of more contemplative compositions that allow the camera to linger and the eye to take in more detail. Wider camera angles welcome props into the frame, situating them among the players like they're important pointers. Delayed cuts encourage us to study the reactions of people left alone in vacated rooms, reading their faces for signals of guilt or innocence like we would a possible suspect's. Sometimes the cuts even lead into dim stairwells or unfrequented passages where secrets collect like dust. The cumulative effect of this shift in editorial technique is the intimation that a plot is being hatched throughout Act II — that we're being presented with clues regarding the culprit, target, and tactics of a nefarious scheme, leaving it up to us to decode the signs and crack the case. As Jobs remarks later in the act, "The plan will reveal itself to you when you're ready to see it." The editing spurs us to look ever closer and be ready.

The film provides plenty of hints as to Jobs' plan, and the setting, San Francisco's War Memorial Opera House, furnishes the first prominent clue. Among the backstage spaces where talent prepares and the front-facing lobbies where audiences confer and gossip, scored by classical-sounding music, the overall agenda is made plain. The first act covers the lead-up to a presentation, but this one presages a *performance* — a practiced set of movements and visuals designed to entrance onlookers, making them forget that what they see onstage is not, in fact, real. Thus, the act telegraphs that the plot at the heart of its mystery rests upon the same sleight-of-hand involved in live theatre or opera. Something is not as it appears — if not some*one*.

This motif develops further in the opera house's orchestra pit, where a confrontation between Jobs and Wozniak is interrupted by talk about the latter's Nixie tube wristwatch. For the earnest, excitable Wozniak, the odd but technologically inventive accessory carries considerable practical utility and happens to double as a fun toy. Yet in the eyes of the exterior-obsessed Jobs, the watch — which requires a screwdriver to adjust and flashes bright, hazard-orange numbers like an improvised countdown timer — is something more incendiary. "You think it looks like a bomb?" asks Wozniak. "Even right now, I'm not a hundred percent sure it isn't," comes the response. The exchange invites us to reconsider what we're looking at in any given moment of Act II. Does form mark function? What are we really seeing? Before the watch scene, Jobs takes pains to explain that the so-called "Black Cube" is not, in truth, a perfect cube; observers only think the machine before them is geometrically uniform. Things are not what they appear at first sight, opening the possibility that people are not who they say they are, either. In this regard, Jobs' bomb comments are less a form of foreshadowing than an outright Chekhov's Gun; by the act's conclusion, something will go off.

Wozniak's attempts to rip away Jobs' mask underscore the second act's theme of hidden roles and functions. "What do you do?" he asks his former partner, after spelling out the many technical and logistical necessities for bringing Apple's computers to life — fields where Jobs' contribution was negligible at best. Jobs responds, "I play the orchestra" — instead of the instruments, he plays the instrumentalists. He does indeed "play" people, but the question is whether they'll be played like an instrument or a patsy. The metaphor clarifies the machinations behind the second act's mystery: somebody is being set up. But, given the specter of failure hovering over the NeXT launch, is Jobs that person?

The latter half of the act stretches that tension, positioning Jobs in an ambiguous role among the trappings of murder scenes, where it's unclear whether he'll be the victim or the perpetrator. Accordingly, his reunion with onetime mentor John Sculley has far darker overtones than any other point in the film. The verb "kill" frequently recurs throughout their conversation. Flashbacks to Jobs' sparse, poorly lit house and the rainy boardroom where Jobs' ouster transpires convey the menacing air of forthcoming violence. Each of the men characterize Jobs' firing from Apple in violent terms, as well — Sculley viewing Jobs' attempted power play as a "suicide," and Jobs dubbing Sculley's successful boardroom gambit a "homicide." Rapid cuts interspersed with uncomfortable flashbacks conjure a mystery movie's climax, where the crime, witnessed in full detail, nears its solution. As Sculley and Jobs argue, the cuts whip back and forth in time from the opera house to the Apple boardroom and back, sentences from the past interrupt utterances in the present, and their voices escalate to outright shouts as the nondiegetic music behind them crescendos. It's the kind of unrestrained emotional outburst that typically accompanies a crime of passion in noir films, and pro-vides a brief glimpse into the volatile mental state that Jobs has spent the entire act disguising. Until the final moments, we're left to wonder who is about to kill whom, how they're going to do it, and why. When the boardroom battle is decided, we find Jobs defeated — ejected from Apple, alienated from friends and former allies, self-image shattered in a way the film has never shown before. By most indications, it seems like Sculley has dealt Jobs a professional deathblow, and NeXT's doomed launch represents his final, staggering steps before irrelevance.

Yet this setup is one last misdirection. For the Sculley scene ultimately reveals not Jobs' murder, but his motive — the trigger for all his plans in the second act. In the final conversation with Hoffman, Jobs parts the curtain: the point of the launch was never to profit off consumers, but for Jobs to sell NeXT's software back to the company that rejected him. And with that, the Chekhov's Gun fires. All at once, Jobs' bizarre computer becomes the inverse of Wozniak's wristwatch, showing itself to be a weapon disguised as a curio. Its ill-advised public unveiling transforms into the elaborate "Steve Jobs Revenge Machine," as Hoffman calls it, whereby Jobs will reclaim Apple by exploiting its brass' weakness and lack of foresight.

Thus, the editing has served to emphasize the story that the script is telling. The dialogue leads us to believe that Jobs is embattled, but all along, he has been exactly where he wants to be. The script may have tricked you into thinking that everything signals his impending collapse, but the editing supplies enough clues to indicate that you've been looking at — and *for* — the wrong thing all along. The plan was always hiding in plain sight; the editing's mystery framing provides the wherewithal to perceive it, and makes its revelation all the more satisfying.

For a few glittering minutes, Act III looks like it will cover Jobs' victory lap. It opens with Jobs onstage, running a dress rehearsal for the latest Apple launch, firmly in his element. The machine Jobs prepares to introduce (the iMac G3, shiny, transparent, and colorful like so many turn-of-the-millennium electronics) is the kind of computer he has dreamed of all throughout the film — built to his specifications, with nobody second-guessing him; instantly appealing to those who behold it; working as intended during the demo. And now, for once, we glimpse a different kind of Jobs, who cracks jokes instead of insults, who elicits laughter rather than unease, whose presence seems softer and less dangerous than before. One hopes that success has mellowed him, allowing him to shed the abrasive behaviors that he had thought necessary to gain and maintain an industry foothold.

Yet this scene is fundamentally a monologue. We hear primarily Jobs' voice, crafting the kind of unchallenged narrative we have heard him trying to spin over and over again. It's not the full picture, as we'll learn soon after other people have had a chance to speak. The image Jobs has cultivated in this moment won't survive contact with reality. And instead of delivering the beatification teased for Jobs in the finale's first moments, Act III brings us to his sentencing.

The third act places us back in the combative register of the film's opening, but with one key difference: the cuts are slower, and rather than follow the rhythm of every rapid-fire riposte, they allow the weight and repercussions of each character's statements to reverberate. This small but meaningful adjustment changes the third act's entire tenor: the film concludes as a drama, and long-telegraphed consequences for Jobs finally arrive. Act III is thus the culmination of a two-pronged tragedy. With career success in hand at last, Jobs is done becoming. But now he must deal with *being*, and since his ambitions have been satisfied, his personal failures are all that is left; success has neither chased them away nor cleansed him of them. His dreams of improving humankind through technology — "a bicycle for the mind" turning man into the planet's most efficient animal — ring hollow when we're confronted with what a dirtbag he has been all along, and still remains; technology has only made him worse, being a vehicle to amplify and justify his monstrosity. He's more than ever a bad father, a selfish prick, and a bottomless well of casual cruelty to those who should be closest to him. The first prong of Jobs' tragedy is that, although one may do questionable things in pursuit of greatness, achievement in itself does not confer redemption.

The shift in attitude toward Jobs is apparent during his final duel with Wozniak. It rehashes the same disagreement from Act I, with Wozniak demanding that

Jobs acknowledge some of Apple's foundational team members during the product launch, and Jobs refusing on the grounds that the launch is about the future instead of the past. Yet this time, the normally gentle Wozniak puts more force into his argument, speaking with a verbal intensity (and an unprecedented hint of vitriol) that indicates he is treating Jobs as a bully to be overpowered rather than a colleague to be persuaded. Meanwhile, the scene is interspersed with cuts showing the Apple employees in the auditorium where Jobs and Wozniak spar — a callback to the shot of the engineering team Jobs assembles backstage in the first act. These onlookers also stand silently watching, but their expressions are noteworthy. Where the employees from the first act appear afraid, concerned that Jobs' lashing tongue will strike them, those in the third look embarrassed, mortified that someone as important as Jobs would create such an awkward situation. We'll see the same reaction among a different set of employees during Jobs' later spat with his daughter, suggesting that this response is now the norm. Splicing in the workers' wordless but judgmental gazes sends a clear message that the Jobs mystique has evaporated in Act III for those who truly know him. Small wonder, then, that Wozniak has the last word in their argument before dismissing him. Nobody fears Jobs anymore, and the old terror he once instilled has been replaced with the secondhand shame one feels when associating with a petulant, irascible elder. Who cares that he helped develop a cool computer if he's liable to make a scene in public?

This new dynamic's implications are made plain in Jobs' last tussles with Hoffman and Hertzfeld. These conversations — concerning Jobs' childish, vindictive refusal to pay his daughter's college tuition — place Jobs on the defensive, limiting his opportunities to parry and counterattack. As with the Wozniak scuffle, the editing in the two conversations adds an important interpretive layer to what is said. The slowed shot cadence focuses on the impact of each character's lines upon their target, rather than immediately pivoting to the recipient's countermove; the emphasis therefore migrates from the linguistic combat itself to its effects. The upshot is that, despite sitting pretty within the wider world of tech, Jobs himself is shown to occupy a weaker position than ever, seeming pathetic to those versed in his tricks and tics. His usual verbal barbs do not land like they used to; where Hoffman and Hertzfeld might have been cowed or deferential in an earlier era, they now more often appear unfazed, and viewers are given plenty of time to internalize those unimpressed reactions. Thus, when Hertzfeld admits to disliking Jobs, and Hoffman notes she can ditch him without personal or professional consequence, these are not cavalier insults discharged in the heat of the moment — they mean what they say, and Jobs cannot compel them to do or think otherwise. And when Jobs is on the receiving end of the others' broadsides, they hit. He's driven into stunned silences, pushed into offering concessions, and more than once shown to cast a wounded glance after a particularly trenchant criticism. The editing presents a Jobs who is forced to reflect instead of deflect, and in those unwelcome intervals, he finds himself as wanting as his interlocutors do.

If the newfound contempt from Jobs' associates signals that past and present alike judge him, the third act furnishes signs that the future also prepares to evaluate him as disdainfully. In one sequence, as Jobs and Hoffman revisit the old *TIME* magazine cover that Jobs found so insulting in Act I, he discovers that the actual image on the cover is not at all what he had thought in 1984 — instead of a person seated before a competing IBM model, it's a sculpture by George Segal of a human figure in front of a generic computer. The sequence captures the arc of Act III in miniature: the future clarifies the past, exposing the failures of intellect and character that Jobs has aggressively tried to paper over. The same dramatic principle is later made manifest through his daughter Lisa, whose scathing reappraisal of Jobs' career previews the future's harsh verdict. For Lisa reminds us that Jobs' machines are not his only testament; there remains his peevish *TIME* interview, along with its ham-fisted and mathematically unsound efforts to deny his daughter's paternity; the cutting remarks from his friends that have been immortalized in print; the court records indicating the paltry financial support he had only reluctantly provided. And, of course, she issues the crushing observation that the cool of today is the cringe of tomorrow, curtly dismissing the iMac G3's painstaking design as *The Jetsons'* take on the Easy-Bake Oven. Lisa's perspective represents the possibility that art is in fact inseparable from the artist, that a work's greatness is only proportional to the smallness of those who made them. "I'm poorly made," Jobs later says, seeking to account for his failures as a parent and person. But this is merely explanatory, not exculpatory — and if all art bears the trace of its creator, the admission implies that Jobs' computers, however thoughtful their construction, all ultimately model his own shortcomings.

The editing, for its part, offers Jobs no absolution. The script hints at a coming reconciliation with Lisa, as if the apologetic tenor of their rooftop conversation and momentary connection in the wings of the presentation stage indicate a change in their relationship. Yet the editing makes sure not to show it. The last we see of Jobs is his blurred outline during the final dissolve, as he crosses the stage amid rapturous applause toward the wing where his daughter stands. Crucially, he never makes it to where Lisa is stationed; the visuals dissipate when he is approximately halfway to stage right. In a way, it's a cruel cut; if this is indeed the birth of a new, more loving Jobs, then that version of him never appears onscreen. But the dissolve invites the audience to question how firmly they believe whether Jobs is even capable of such a transformation. When he shows Lisa the printout of the digital painting she made as a child, do you truly buy that he treasures it because it's hers, and not because it's a testament to the art his genius inspires? When Jobs walks toward her in the final seconds, maybe he's simply following a blocking plan that places him at stage right, and his daughter remains an afterthought now that the product launch is underway. The entire film up to now has involved people finding out that Jobs' motives are always selfish, and his few kindnesses — such as they are — incidental. Why, at this point, should we expect him to move for anyone but himself?

The editing does not allow Jobs his redemption, because he has not earned it. But his failure in this regard is not what gives *Steve Jobs* a tragic ending. Herein lies the second prong of Act III's tragedy, and the film's more broadly: That, even once Jobs' irredeemable character is made plain, there remain auditoriums packed full of people who believe that he and his like are worthy of adulation.

Ladies and gentlemen, Steve Jobs.

Aftermath

by B.C. Wallin

There's a poster I've been holding onto: white background. A contemplative figure in black and white. Lowercase title in Helvetica type. I think a lot about *Steve Jobs*, the movie I've seen more than any other. A poster is not a movie, but it's a way to try and hold onto it. Like quoting, making memes, or buying a Blu-ray. You try to hang on, but things slip away.

Imagine this. There's a video shop in your mind where you walk across the drab gray carpeting, past the laminated VHS and DVD cases of every movie you've ever considered. Of course, there are the Movies You Must Watch and the Movies Everyone Has Watched in the most prominent displays. Nearby are the Movies Everyone's Talking About Right Now — last year's collection has already entered the bargain bin. But you're past the prestige entrance, with its cardboard cutouts and movie snacks; now your eyes scan more shelves as you plunge further.

Here are the Movies Your Friends Told You To Watch Ages Ago. Below them are the Movies You Said You'd Watch When They Were In Theaters, But By Now Have Lost The Energy To Try. There, beautifully displayed, are the Movies You Think About Because Of

Their Gorgeous Posters. So, too, the Movies You Wish Were More Deserving Of Their Gorgeous Posters. Below the flickering fluorescents you see them, the Movies You'd Watch But Are Waiting To Watch In Order, the Great Movies You've Seen side-by-side with their Lesser Sequels You'd Get Around To If Not For Really Poor Receptions. The Movies That You Used To Enjoy But Honestly It's Just Getting Annoying Because There's So Many Of Them And Everyone Who Ever Talks About Them Completely Sours Your Relationship With Them. You tilt one off the shelf, you put it back. You wonder about the ethics of choosing one over the other, justifying yourself when there's nobody you have to justify yourself to.

If you're like me or my wife, you have the One Movie You Keep Coming Back To. The one that's like the proverbial river that the same proverbial man can't come to twice. Or maybe it's like a shrine you visit on your pilgrimage, annually or otherwise. These movies form unique relationships with us. When my wife was younger and going to the video shop that wasn't in her mind, she'd run down the ramp, find the old familiar spot, and rent *Thumbelina* every time. I asked why her family never just bought the VHS, and I never got a good answer.

The shops have closed down or become Airbnbs, but our relationship to film doesn't change. Every movie is a rental. When we turn it on, it's ours. And then the lights come on, the projector whirs to a halt, or the DVD ejects, or the streaming service asks us what we'd like to watch next. Movies live, move, and exist when we watch them, and then the illusion is over and they're back to being VHS covers in our minds, dead objects in shells or cans or ever-shifting databases of content — just the idea of a movie, until the pictures are in motion again. So those of us who've found love or fascination or magic keep renting them and renewing. We keep up our resurrection act, bringing these films back to life, renting them enough that it feels like we own the things.

There are those rare films, the ones that feel like nobody else could possibly have seen them as much as you have. You own it; it's yours. By watching something enough times — by talking about it, posting, thinking, subsuming — you become one body with that film. It's yours and you are its. Usually, this happens with the underloved, overhated films, torn apart by the wide world and beloved by the few and the devoted. Or else, with the obscure, underseen movies, the ones that you've never heard another soul mention, unless you told them first.

It's also possible to feel this devotion to the movies that came and went within their limited lifespan. The shelves are teeming, the options continue to feel endless. And once a film no longer seems relevant or like it's part of the cultural conversation, it's easy to let it get piled behind all the other Movies That Have Been On Your Watchlist For Too Long. So sometimes, you latch onto one that wasn't considered bad and may have even gotten critical acclaim and awards acknowledgements, but which has otherwise disappeared. I know I have.

*
**

In 2015, I saw the movie *Steve Jobs* one time. I woke up on a Sunday afternoon and my mom asked me if I wanted to do something together. As I usually did, I checked the theater showtimes and noticed that the Steve Jobs movie was out. I'd liked the figure of Steve Jobs for some time and thought the movie might be interesting. We saw it, it confused me, it reminded me of *The Social Network*, and we went home.

In 2016, I saw the movie *Steve Jobs* zero times.

In 2017, I saw the movie *Steve Jobs* zero times.

In 2018, I saw or listened to the movie *Steve Jobs* some 20 or 30 times. I'd come across YouTube clips of fast talking, sharp editing, and bold music, and I started watching them over and over again. I came to the movie for the first time in three years and then I came to it again and I came to it again. I'd finish watching it and start over immediately. I downloaded the movie on my phone so I could listen to it on the subway. I saw references to the movie everywhere, even if they weren't really there. I watched the movie wherever I went. I got married. I kept watching it.

Being consumed by a film is like learning a new vocabulary word: you start to notice it in every sentence, you find yourself referencing it often. Too often. Oh, that actor played Steve Jobs' daughter in one segment of the movie. Paul Rand? I heard his name in a throwaway line. And here's a movie rife with throwaway lines — it's writer Aaron Sorkin's style to try to elevate his work with references to better art, including (elsewhere) *Don Quixote*, a work that opens with a prologue concerning books so full of unnecessary references "that they amaze their readers, who consider the authors to be well-read, erudite and eloquent men."

I'd tell my friends that I'd watched *Steve Jobs* again. They'd ask why I was so consumed by such a culturally unremarkable thing, and quickly add that they didn't really want a reason. It wouldn't matter. The movie came. It went. It earned two Oscar nominations and a disappointing box office return.

By the time 2015 ended, it should have been relegated to the past, right? *Steve Jobs* was a movie that existed to be compared to another Steve Jobs movie, never to exist on its own. A movie with hot-button discussions about insulting Apple and the family of Steve Jobs, it was perfect for *Deadline* articles about squabbles, and Jimmy Kimmel and Stephen Colbert appearances with brash statements and apologies. This is how most movies that make any impact now live: announcement, discussion, cast photos, controversies, trailers, reviews, backlash, backlash, backlash, different reviews, the movie comes out, and within two weeks, we can let it go and move on to the next thing. Check what's in the theater this weekend, roll out of bed, start again. Danny Boyle and Aaron Sorkin go on to direct movies that get forgotten. What else can we watch?

But why watch anything else?

Like a musical without song, *Steve Jobs* is all rhythm and cadence, interplay and harmony. It's a symphony of voices, all at odds with each other. Watch the film and then listen to composer Daniel Pemberton's score; there's something missing from the synthesized, orchestral, and computer-designed arrangements. Vocal lashings punctuate the movie with the kind of precision that Sorkin's works have become infamous for. With enough viewings, the film becomes a choreographed work of sparring partners hitting their marks and delivering their lines with a precise bite and venom.

I was captivated by the musicality of the language, by the sharp wit that sounds as if everyone is either the smartest person in the world or has been training for weeks at a time for the arguments they're in. The more I watched *Steve Jobs*, the more I realized how much it tapped into everything I found fascinating about the person who inspired the movie — he just kept pulling off his magic tricks. A computer so thin, it fit in a manila envelope. A music player so small, you could keep it in the small pocket of your jeans. Three revolutionary devices that were actually a single powerhouse called iPhone. And they all came with the magic words: "It just works." Here was a movie that didn't show any of those inventions, yet fully understood the value of the trick. Even if it didn't understand the technology behind it, it understood the value of the showman, the magnetic Jobs personality.

Steve Jobs (Michael Fassbender) is the focal point of

Steve Jobs. Which is not to say simply that he's the subject. Within the view of the camera, he's the point of refraction and reflection. He's the center of all. The camera tracks him through hallway and stairwell. It crouches with, closes in on, and revolves around him. He's the sun, and everyone else his minor planets and moons in orbit. Everyone other than Jobs is in the periphery, in one way or another. We so rarely leave the man, and when we do, it's only to see those straining to leave his gravity or mesmerized by the spell of his brightness.

He cannot help but control the soundtrack of his reality, too. There are moments of reflection, where he seems to enter a trance, and Pemberton's score goes along with him. The endlessly urging momentum slows, and the entire atmosphere is suffused with an externalized anguish that we must feel along with Jobs. His ecstasy inflates a room with triumph, his impatience ticks wildly, and his tenseness holds everyone in its grip. And then, there's the one musical hint that maybe he's been behind it all, when he cues the score with a clap.

Even the structures he resides in cannot escape his controlling hand. Bob Dylan lyrics take over the floor as Jobs reconsiders which quote to reference in his keynote. He tells a story about Skylab and the satellite blasts across the wall of a hallway. As Jobs transitions between sections of the movie, the material of reality changes with him. The 16mm film runs out at the end of 1984, the 35mm reel gets unspooled as 1988 concludes, and in the introduction to 1998, the HD footage briefly pixelates. Jobs evolves, and the medium must shift along with him.

When he's not unconsciously manipulating his environment, Jobs does it at will. He tinkers with lighting and wardrobe. He makes last-minute adjustments on a whim. In '84, he changes his shirt so that he can pull off the magic trick of pulling a computer program out of his breast pocket. In '88, he grabs calla lilies from the San Francisco Opera House restaurant to replace the flowers on display with his computer. In '98, he's still tinkering with which picture of a shark will accompany a joke in his keynote later that day. At every moment, Jobs is either controlling or wishing he could be. He's magnetic, he's manipulative, he's at the center of everything that sparkles and captivates in *Steve Jobs*.

I've watched him so much.

Plenty of movies reach the end of their lifespans before we've even started to find what makes them great. They don't have a shelf life. They disappear from consciousness and we each feel like we're the only ones trying to bring them to life. We may try to capture or approach them by filling our folders with screenshots and GIFs, our displays with cutesy versions of movie figures, or our shelves with beautifully designed home media releases, finding a way to spare the movies from death in some way. They begin to develop a new life in physical mementos, references, writings, and memories of special screenings, but the leftover traces of a movie never do fully add up to the movie itself. We rent these movies and bring them back to the store in our minds, and come back later to find them exactly where we left them.

Orson Welles once said, "Film is a dead thing — a ribbon of celluloid — like the paper on which one writes a poem." Years later, when asked about the quote, he added, "You don't get anything back from the audience; [film] can't nourish itself on that audience. A movie doesn't come to life *because* it's in a theatre." And while film may remain unchanging, stuck in the past — like *Psycho*'s Marion Crane, doomed to die no matter how many times we watch her — I beg to differ with Welles. The life of a movie must come precisely from the audience; without being perceived by one, a film might as well be a dead flounder for all the good it does sitting in a can. When the lights go down and the movie plays, a film comes to life. Movies live while we watch them, in their movement and — when shot on film, and crystals of silver salts being exposed to light turn into dye clouds that create the speckled movement we call film grain — in the physical materials they're made of.

Two-thirds of *Steve Jobs* was shot on film, but the grain — evocative as it is of the eras and their technology — is not what brings it to life for me. Every time I replay the movie, I keep going back to the musicality. Sorkin often talks about the music of the scene being what he's looking for. Of one particularly difficult segment to bring to life, Sorkin said, "It wasn't singing yet." Whenever I listen to Pemberton's wonderfully creative score — like the film stock, it changes in each era, in style and instrumentation — it feels like it's missing something. The dialogue is all part of the tone of the film, and even listening to *Steve Jobs* with no visuals can be like the experience of listening to a great album. Sure, it's spoken word mixed with orchestral or electronic music, but it sings.

I've read the screenplay, but often my mind wanders back to the sound and the music. Michael Fassbender didn't try to imitate Jobs, but his line deliveries are fascinating. I'd keep getting hooked on the way he says, "They won't know what they're looking at or why they like it, but they'll know they want it," or the way Kate Winslet drops an exasperated Polish "Jesus Christ" in the classic Sorkin so-fast-you'll-miss-what-they're-actually-saying first scene. It's like having a song stuck in your head, but nobody gets how you learned the words or why you're singing along in the first place.

Steve Jobs was my go-to. My old familiar. Mine. That's how I felt. You watch the rental enough times and think you can get away with not returning it to the store. You'll pay the missing movie fee and just quietly hold onto the copy that nobody else wanted anyway. Maybe this movie could belong to me. After all, I'm the one keeping it alive, aren't I? That's probably arrogance speaking. Nobody owns a movie, not even the people who made it.

A movie is. It exists, ready to be brought to life, to be appreciated by someone, anyone. Since 2018, that was my relationship with *Steve Jobs*, a movie I wouldn't shut up about because it never stopped speaking to me. Pretty much every year, when the best-of lists come out and the ranking begins, I revisit Roger Ebert's own top-ten list, where he writes, "If I must make a list of the Ten Greatest Films of All Time, my first vow is to make the list for myself, not for anybody else." He argues that the greatest movies appeal to emotions and are the ones that make us feel, "and so my greatest films must be films that had me sitting transfixed before the screen, involved, committed, and feeling." A movie like *Steve Jobs*, that held onto me and wouldn't let go, forcing me to revisit and re-enter its living, breathing, heightened reality. A work of collaboration and auteurship, a vision of an icon of the past via image-making of the future, an opera without song, a work of risk-taking and innovation and challenge and disappointment. If a movie can escape a seemingly inevitable death with such insistence, why wouldn't I hold right back on?

So I held on. And I held on some more. I might have started to let go by now. Eventually it's time to go back to the shelves. What else is there to see?

Sources

Steve Jobs by Walter Isaacson, Simon & Schuster, 2011
Steve Jobs, directed by Danny Boyle, 2015
Steve Jobs: Shooting Script by Aaron Sorkin, March 19,
    2015

Production

"Steve Jobs obituary" by Jack Schofield, *The Guardian*,
    October 5, 2011
"Jobs' Biography: Thoughts On Life, Death And
    Apple," *NPR*, October 25, 2011
"Sony Pictures Acquiring New Steve Jobs Biography
    For Major Feature Film" by Mike Fleming, Jr.,
    Deadline, October 7, 2011
"A Widow's Threats, High-Powered Spats and the Sony
    Hack: The Strange Saga of 'Steve Jobs'" by Stephen
    Galloway, *The Hollywood Reporter*, October 7, 2015
"Noah Wyle on playing Steve Jobs," *Fortune*, October 7,
    2011
"Apple Opens Up to Praise New Book on Steve Jobs,
    and Criticize an Old One" by Brian X. Chen and
    Alexandra Alter, *The New York Times*, March 22,
    2015
"Will Aaron Sorkin take on Steve Jobs?" by Steven
    Zeitchik, *Los Angeles Times*, October 25, 2011
"Hi. It's Steve." by Aaron Sorkin, *Newsweek*, October
    10, 2011

"Aaron Sorkin talked to a key person in Steve Jobs' life whom even Jobs' biographer couldn't get to — and it changed the whole script of his movie" by Jason Guerrasio, *Business Insider*, October 7, 2015

"Ashton Kutcher to Play Steve Jobs in Indie Biopic" by Pamela McClintock, *Variety*, April 1, 2012

"Sorkin says Jobs movie won't be straight biography" reported by Jill Serjeant, *Reuters*, May 18, 2012

"Leonardo DiCaprio Exits Steve Jobs Biopic as Contenders Line Up (Exclusive)" by Tatiana Siegel & Borys Kit, *The Hollywood Reporter*, October 2, 2014

"The Sony Hack and the Yellow Press" by Aaron Sorkin, *The New York Times*, December 14, 2014

"Universal Picks Up Steve Jobs Movie" by Gregg Kilday, *The Hollywood Reporter*, November 24, 2014

"'Steve Jobs' Cast Finalized, Finally, As Shooting Begins," *Deadline*, January 27, 2015

"Danny Boyle's Portrait of a Man" by Emma Brown, *Interview Magazine*, October 19, 2015

"Michael Fassbender: Memorizing *Steve Jobs* Was Harder Than Shakespeare" by Eliza Berman, *TIME*, February 26, 2016

"Production Information: *Steve Jobs*," Universal Studios, September 14, 2015

"NYFF: 'Steve Jobs' Star Michael Fassbender, Director Danny Boyle Weren't Bothered by Pre-Production Drama" by Hilary Lewis, *The Hollywood Reporter*, October 4, 2015

"How Kate Winslet Won a Role in Steve Jobs and Managed All That Sorkin Dialogue" by Boris Kachka,

Vulture, August 26, 2015

"Inside Jobs: The Making of *Steve Jobs*," 2016

"STEVE JOBS" by Guy Hendrix Dyas, Susie Alegria, Peter Borck, Luke Freeborn, and Emily Rolph, *Perspective*, November-December 2015

"Contender - Production Designer Guy Hendrix Dyas, Steve Jobs" by Jack Egan, *Below the Line*, January 4, 2016

"How I was almost a Steve Jobs movie extra" by Shara Tibken, *CNET*, February 3, 2015

"I was an extra in the 'Steve Jobs' movie" by Roman Loyola, *MacWorld*, February 3, 2015

"'Steve Jobs' movie: A backstage look at a backstage drama" by David Ng, *Los Angeles Times*, October 26, 2015

"A Total System Reboot" by Geoffrey Haley, *Camera Operator*, Fall 2015

"Interview with Susan Kare" by Alex Pang, *Making the Macintosh: Technology and Culture in Silicon Valley*, Stanford University, February 19, 2001

With acknowledgement to JJ Bersch and Alice Wasley for supplying some of the sources used.

Jobs

"Here's how much Steve Jobs used to obsess over presentations" by Jillian D'Onfro, *Business Insider*, March 29, 2015

Revolution in the Valley by Andy Hertzfeld, O'Reilly, 2004

"How Steve Jobs Made Presentations Look Effortless" by Carmine Gallo, *Forbes*, March 26, 2015

"Steve on Stage," allaboutSteveJobs.com

"The Steve Jobs You Never Saw: An Exploration of His Unexpected Sartorial Choices," *Julien's Auctions*, October 23, 2014

Make Something Wonderful, edited by Leslie Berlin, Steve Jobs Archive, 2023

"'Steve Jobs' Costume Designer – Suttirat Larlarb – In Conversation," *Film Doctor*, December 1, 2015

"Understanding Steve Jobs' Design Philosophy: How Form Met Function," *PressFarm*, October 2, 2025

"Khadi – Indian Hand Spinning And Weaving: Tradition, Innovation, And Sustainability," *Textile School*, March 11, 2025

"Indian Fabric: Khadi – Handwoven Tradition & Craftsmanship," *Fibre Bio*, August 23, 2019

"Kantha: The Story," House of Wandering Silk

Sorkin

"Notes on the Auteur Theory in 1962" by Andrew Sarris, *Film Culture*, Winter 1962/63

A Few Good Men: Revised Third Draft by Aaron Sorkin, July 15, 1991

The Social Network: Screenplay by Aaron Sorkin

Boyle

Trainspotting, directed by Danny Boyle, 1996

"Gregory and the Heptarchs: The Christianization of
    Anglo-Saxon England" by Charles J. Lockett,
    Medieval Ware, October 25, 2021

"Ridley Scott: 'I'm doing pretty good, if you think about
    it'" by James Mottram, *The Independent*, September
    3, 2010

"Danny Boyle Launches Pioneering £35m School of
    Digital Arts in Manchester," *I Love MCR*, June 15,
    2022

Camera

Side by Side, directed by Christopher Kenneally, 2012

"*28 Days Later*: All the Rage" by Douglas Bankston,
    American Cinematographer, July 2021

"Anthony Dod Mantle, DFF injects the apocalyptic *28
    Days Later* with a strain of digital video." by Douglas
    Bankston, *American Cinematographer*, July 2003

"*Sunshine*: Let There Be Light" by Jay Holben,
    American Cinematographer, March 25, 2021

"Rags to Riches" by Stephanie Argy, *American
    Cinematographer*, December 2008

"No Fear: Anthony Dod Mantle DFF BSC / *127 Hours,
    The Eagle & Dredd 3D*" by Ron Prince, *British
    Cinematographer*, May 2015

"*127 Hours:* Up Against It" by Mark Hope-Jones,
    American Cinematographer, December 2010

"*Steve Jobs*: Thinking Different" by Noah Kadner,
    American Cinematographer, November 2015

"Apple Core: Alwin Küchler BSC / *Steve Jobs*," *British
    Cinematographer*, February 2016

Steve Jobs Commentary by Danny Boyle, Universal
    Pictures, 2016

"Why Danny Boyle used iPhones on 28 Years Later" by
    Maati Haapoja, June 18, 2015

"Anthony Dod Mantle on Shooting '28 Years Later'
    With iPhones, Drones & Danny Boyle's Demands,"
    HeyUGuys, June 18, 2015

"'The Phones Became Weapons': Anthony Dod Mantle
    on Animating *28 Years Later* with Danny Boyle" by
    Nick Newman, *The Film Stage*, June 19, 2025

Music

"Daniel Pemberton on Composing the Score for 'Steve
    Jobs'" by Nell Minow, *Huffington Post*, October 13,
    2015

"How Composer Daniel Pemberton Created 3 Scores
    for *Steve Jobs*" by Alice Wasley, *The Credits*,
    November 2, 2015

"STEVE JOBS Composer Daniel Pemberton on Creating a
    Score Reflective of Steve Jobs' Life and Career" by
    Kiko Martinez, *Tribeca*, October 22, 2015

"Why Is the Steve Jobs Movie So Obsessed with Bob
    Dylan?" by Zach Schonfeld, *Newsweek*, October 16,
    2015

"A Symphony in Three Parts: Breaking Down the 'Steve

Jobs' Score with Composer Daniel Pemberton,"
    PopMatters, November 13, 2015
Steve Jobs Commentary by Aaron Sorkin and Elliot
    Graham, Universal Pictures, 2016
"Daniel Pemberton: Scoring Steve Jobs" by Paul
    Weedon, *Clash Music*, November 18, 2015

Edit

"'Steve Jobs' editor – Elliot Graham – In Conversation"
    by Andy Wooding, *Film Doctor*, December 8, 2015
"Editing 'Steve Jobs' - Variety Artisans" by David S.
    Cohen, *Variety*, November 3, 2015
Raging Bull, directed by Martin Scorsese, 1980

Aftermath

*A version of this essay was published as "Steve Jobs: The
    Lifespan of a Film" on Bright Wall/Dark Room on
    November 4, 2022.*

Don Quixote by Miguel De Cervantes Saavedra,
    translated by John Rutherford, Penguin Classics,
    2003
"The Cinema of Orson Welles" by Peter Bogdanovich,
    The Film Library of the Museum of Modern Art,
    1961
This Is Orson Welles by Orson Welles & Peter
    Bogdanovich, Hachette Books, 1998
"Aaron Sorkin Walks (And Talks) Us Through His Best
    Dialogue Scenes" by Emma Thrower, *Empire*,

November 9, 2015
"Ten Greatest Films of All Time" by Roger Ebert,
RogerEbert.com, December 19, 2012

Contributors

Charlie Brigden is a writer based in South Wales in the UK, who has written about film music for two decades. Their work has been featured on records by Mondo, Sony Classical, and Mutant, and they have written regularly for the likes of *Roger Ebert* and *The Quietus*. Their first Apple product was a sixth-generation silver iPod Classic.

Alexander B. Joy is the author of *Legend of the River King* (Boss Fight Books, 2026) and the editor of *Flaxman Low: Occult Detective* (MIT Press, 2026). Find him on Bluesky at @aeneas-nin.bsky.social, and see more of his work at alexanderbjoy.com.

Sarah Jae Leiber is a southpaw from Philadelphia with a soft spot for Milo Ventimiglia, just like Rocky Balboa. Criticism: *NPR, Polygon, Bitch, Bright Wall/Dark Room, Jewish Women's Archive*. Her plays have been performed at McCarter, Theatre Row, Muhlenberg College, Actors Theatre of Louisville, The Tank, and more. Her first Apple product was a first-generation iPad.

Aashima Rawal is a freelance writer and author whose work explores the intersections of art, history, and storytelling. Her essays have appeared in *Art UK, Hearth Magazine*, and *Futbolista*. She focuses on bringing cultural narratives to life through accessible, research-driven writing. Her first Apple product was a second-generation silver iPod Touch.

Devan Scott is a cinematographer, colourist, educator, and occasional director. He holds a BFA in Film Production from Simon Fraser University, teaches at the University of British Columbia, Emily Carr University, and Emerson College, and hosts the podcasts *Film Formally* and *How Would Lubitsch Do It*.

Scout Tafoya is a filmmaker, author, critic, and video essayist from Doylestown, PA. His first Apple product was a fourth-generation iPod.

Kat Trout-Baron is a first-year Screenwriting MFA candidate at the American Film Institute. They received a BA in Screenwriting and Cinema from the University of Iowa. Their writing has appeared in conference at the University of Indiana and at FilmScene, a non-profit cinema where Trout-Baron served as a student programmer. Their first Apple product was a first-generation silver iPod Touch.

B.C. Wallin is a writer and sometimes critic whose work can be found in such places as *Bright Wall/Dark Room*, *Polygon*, *Vulture*, *Little White Lies*, and *Broad Sound*. He is the creator and editor of *STEVE JOBS MONOGRAPH*, his first film book. His first Apple product was a second-generation green iPod Nano.